O/L 14/9 G.

In replying to this letter, please w...

Number 8078 Name R.us...

H.M. PRISON,
JEBB AVENUE,
BRIXTON,
LONDON, S.W.2

..................................Prison

Sp. 15, 1961

My Darling

The lawyer's nice young man brought me cheering news of you & told me I could write to you, which I had not known. Every one here treats me kindly & the only thing I mind is being away from you. At all odd minutes I have the illusion that you are there, & forget that if I sneeze it won't disturb you. I am enjoying Madame de Staël immensely, having at last got round to reading her. At odd moments I argue theology with the chaplain & medicine with the Doctor, & so the time passes easily. But separation from you is quite horrid, Dearest Love, it will be heavenly when we are together again. Take care of yourself, Beloved.

B.

The Spokesman
Keep the Peace
Edited by Tony Simpson
Published by Spokesman for the
Bertrand Russell Peace Foundation
Ken Coates: Editor 1970 to 2010

Spokesman 143   2019

Subscriptions
Institutions £40.00 (ex UK)
£33.00 (UK)
Individuals £20.00 (UK)
£25.00 (ex UK)

A CIP catalogue record for this book is available from the British Library

CONTENTS

Editorial	3		
Appointment in Tehran	5	*Pugwash*	
Iran Alert	15	*Bertrand Russell Peace Foundation*	
Plan for Iran	19	*Tom Unterrainer*	
Chemical Weapons	27	*Helena Cobban*	
Australia and the Bomb	33	*Cmdr Robert Forsyth*	
Hiroshima Declaration	36	*Kazumi Matsui*	
Chernobyl	39	*Zhores Medvedev*	
Agbogbloshie Blues	49	*Gregory Woods*	
Working with Bertie	50	*Ken Coates*	
Before CND	65	*Peggy Duff & Ken Blackwell*	
Byron and the Byronic	75	*Bertrand Russell*	
Letter to Oswald Mosley	91	*Bertrand Russell*	
Inside the Goldmine	93	*Daniel Jakopovich*	
Focus on Europe	101	*John McDonnell MP*	
NPT Dossier	103	*Iran, China*	
Reviews	114	*Barry Baldwin, Stephen Winfield, Anthony Lane*	

Published by
The Bertrand Russell Peace Foundation Ltd,
5 Churchill Park,
Nottingham, NG4 2HF
England
Tel. 0115 9708318
email: editor@russfound.org
www.spokesmanbooks.com
www.russfound.org

Editorial Board
John Daniels
Ken Fleet
Stuart Holland
Henry McCubbin
Abi Rhodes
Regan Scott
Tom Unterrainer

FSC
Mixed Sources
Product group from well-managed forests and other controlled sources
Cert no. SGS-COC-006541
www.fsc.org
© 1996 Forest Stewardship Council

Cover: Bertrand and Edith Russell, London, 1961
Sally and Richard Greenhill/Alamy Stock Photos

ISSN 1367 7748   ISBN 978 0 85124 8820

Editorial

Keep the Peace

At 3pm on Saturday 18 February 1961, 'the quietist, most orderly, most impressive mass demonstration senior police officers could recall' marched in silence down Whitehall and sat outside the Ministry of Defence for two-and-a-half hours. Whilst there, Bertrand Russell with others taped a declaration on the door of the Ministry demanding 'immediate scrapping of the agreement to base Polaris-carrying submarines in Britain,' concluding, 'we hereby serve notice on our Government that we no longer stand aside while they prepare to destroy mankind'. 'Reporters had to squat down beside Lord Russell and his companions to gather their stories,' according to Christopher Driver in his informative and entertaining book, *The Disarmers*, published in 1964. 'The press was sympathetic.'

Subsequently, US President Kennedy told British Prime Minister Macmillan that the United States would sell to Britain the Polaris nuclear missiles, armed with nuclear warheads manufactured in the UK, so long as the nuclear weapons remained, at least nominally, a NATO capacity. That deadly arrangement endures.

What happened meanwhile? The next big sit-down was in Parliament Square on 29 April 1961. The police removed 826 demonstrators, most of whom were fined £1 and allowed seven days to pay, so that the prisons were not overwhelmed.

Thereafter, parallel demonstrations were planned for Holy Loch in Scotland, where the Polaris submarines were to be based, and for Central London on 17 September, Battle of Britain Sunday. 'During the first week of September, the Government did the one thing needful to ensure a good turn-out,' according to Driver. 'It summoned 36 of the better known members of the Committee [of 100], including Lord and Lady Russell, and invited them at Bow Street to bind themselves over under the 1361 Act to keep the peace for one year.' The Russells were among 32 of 36 who refused to be so bound and, to cries of 'shame', they were sentenced to two months in prison. The Russells' sentences were reduced to one week for medical reasons, while others were imprisoned for longer. The subsequent

◄ *Russell's letter to his wife Edith from Brixton Prison*

turbulent Trafalgar Square sit-down on Battle of Britain Sunday marked the 'high tide of unconstitutionalism', in Driver's estimation. Some 4,000 police arrested 1,314 people, including Canon Collins, CND's Chairman, and Fenner Brockway MP. At Holy Loch, 351 people were arrested.

In this issue of *The Spokesman*, to mark the 50th anniversary of Russell's death in February 1970, Ken Coates revisits the enduring issues of civil disobedience when reflecting on his own experience of working with Russell during the last years of Bertie's long life. It will soon be 10 years since Ken died in 2010. Peggy Duff, CND's first general secretary, recalls those times in discussion with Ken Blackwell, the Russell Archivist at McMaster University, Canada, where Bertie's extensive papers are meticulously held.

What are the lessons for today? We live in tumultuous, climate changing times. In the 1930s, Russell alongside many others warned of the dangers of rising fascism. Characteristically, he sought its roots when giving the Byron Lecture in Nottingham, which we reprint here.

Bertrand Russell died on 2 February 1970, in his 98th year. Fifty years on, he sells tens of thousands of books in all formats, while new translations of his works continue to appear around the world, recently in the Arabic, Chinese, Russian and Spanish languages. His reputation as a philosopher and mathematician endures and grows, with young researchers into Artificial Intelligence revisiting *Principia Mathematica* and related works. Meanwhile, Facebook pages in his name attract hundreds of thousands of followers. Russell's life and work speak to people across the generations. The Bertrand Russell Society, founded in 1974, brings together people interested in all aspects of Russell's life and work, and promotes the causes he championed. Its motto, following Russell, is this:

The good life is one inspired by love and guided by knowledge

※ ※ ※

No war on Iran

The Joint Comprehensive Plan of Action addresses long-term tensions in the Middle East, where Israel is probably the sole nuclear-armed state. Signed in 2015 by China, France, Germany, Iran, Russia, UK, US and the High Representative of the European Union, the plan is badly undermined by the US withdrawal. We examine the context and consequences of this violation.

Appointment in Tehran

Pugwash

In June 2019, representatives of Pugwash Conferences on Science and World Affairs initiated a roundtable debate on the threats to the international agreement on Iran's nuclear activities. Poul Erik Christiansen of Pugwash prepared this report, which reflects a diversity of contributions.

On 23-24 June 2019, a delegation from Pugwash travelled to Iran to participate in a specially arranged two day meeting organised together with the Institute for Political and International Studies (IPIS) in Tehran. The central focus of the discussions was the current status of the Joint Comprehensive Plan of Action (JCPOA), more than a year after the United States withdrew from implementing it, and the ensuing programme of ever tightening sanctions imposed by the United States on Iran that has dramatically increased tension in the Middle East. The meeting also put this into context by looking at the regional situation of arms control, as well as Iran's relations with China, Russia, the European Union, and its neighbours including Afghanistan.

Summary of key points

- With so-called 'secondary sanctions' applied by the US against other countries and businesses for trading with Iran, we are at a unique point in United Nations history where countries are being punished for upholding a UN Security Council Resolution (2231).

- The recent resumption of nuclear activities by Iran, in disagreement with the limits set by the JCPOA, is the result of an internal domestic compromise following the year of 'strategic patience' that brought no results in sanctions relief.

- The steps taken by Iran are viewed

in reaction to the US withdrawal from the JCPOA and the lack of EU action since. It was stated several times that each step has been relatively small and is reversible.

- Iran is adamant that these steps are legal remedial measures, well within their right according to the Dispute Resolution Mechanism of the JCPOA outlined in paragraphs 36 and 37.

- The overwhelming emphasis of Iranian sentiment is that it is incumbent on the EU to make progress in providing sanctions relief according to the terms of the JCPOA. The main issue for Iran is to grant the capability of selling oil.

- If steps are not taken soon by the EU and US to address the economic obligations toward Iran under the JCPOA then the regional situation will continue to deteriorate dramatically.

- Further regional instability can provoke dangerous attitudes in other regional actors, particularly with respect to the Nuclear Non-Proliferation Treaty.

- On the current path, an Iranian exit from the NPT may become a possibility, even though Iranian authorities are far from keen to take this step which would serve only to promote a regional arms race.

- All countries must understand that the development of a civilian nuclear programme without a serious system of international control will always create ambiguity with respect to possible military dimensions.

Introduction

Iranian participants made clear that they hear the drumbeat of war. Recent American policy and actions were perceived as intent upon provoking conflict, but the assumption that regime change within Iran would follow from military strikes was seen as deeply misplaced. Similarly, the notion that President Trump's stated 'economic warfare' campaign would cause a collapse of Iran was seen as based upon poor and misleading information provided by regional actors. Rather, it was viewed as an economic war against ordinary Iranians that has not only unified the country against the sanctions but could result in stricter economic and political control for hardliners in Iran. There was a strong sentiment that US allies in the region had felt that the original negotiation and implementation of the JCPOA would lead to an acceptance and integration of Iran into the world economy that would threaten their own interests. They have thus been seeking to undermine and ultimately destroy the nuclear deal not based upon the non-proliferation merits of the JCPOA but on a logic of regional and international geopolitical competition.

US withdrawal from the JCPOA

At the time of the meeting, more than 400 days had passed since the US withdrew from implementing its obligations under the JCPOA, thereby violating both the nuclear deal and the UNSCR 2231. Participants viewed the US decision as being based on erroneous assumptions, in particular a misperception of their own interests, as well as those of their principal regional ally, Israel. Moreover, the notion that a 'better deal' was, and still is, available was viewed as a mistake, and a recent swell of American opinion that Iran should remain in the JCPOA was seen to reveal that across the board many now realize this to be true. Most Iranians were clear that they do not see any prospect of a new deal or of re-opening the JCPOA for re-negotiation; given the years of negotiation to reach the JCPOA it cannot simply be replaced by a 'two-page document'.

In spite of the re-imposition of US nuclear-related sanctions, as well as the punitive array of further sanctions, the International Atomic Energy Agency had verified Iran's continued compliance with the nuclear deal 16 times up to 31 May 2019.

The Iranian policy of 'strategic patience' following the announced US withdrawal in May 2018 was intended to provide the remaining partners to the JCPOA time to deliver upon the agreement and thereby enforce the deal as it was originally defined. This Iranian decision was said to be a 'domestic compromise' among the different factions of the political system, some of whom were firmly against the JCPOA itself and even advocated withdrawal from the Nuclear non-Proliferation Treaty (NPT). Nevertheless, most Iranians believed that remaining in the JCPOA was in Iran's interests in the long run, as well as those of the international community, but noted that without receiving the economic benefits that were part of the compromise there is little clear incentive to remain in the deal.

All participants were in agreement that the US withdrawal constitutes a violation of the JCPOA and UNSCR 2231. It was noted that we are now in a situation where, with so-called 'secondary sanctions' (or 'extra-territorial' sanctions) applied by the US against other countries and businesses for trading with Iran, we are at a unique point in United Nations history where countries are being punished for upholding a UN Security Council Resolution. European banks and businesses have abandoned Iran, and had it not been for ongoing Chinese and Russian activity, it was said that Iran would have left the JCPOA one year ago. One well-informed participant stated that globally all countries have decreased their trade volume with Iran in the past year, with the exception of one: the US has flouted its own sanctions regime but curiously increased its trade with Iran (primarily agricultural products sold to Iran). In sum, current US actions and policy were seen as dangerous and potentially devastating for the region as a whole, and in particular for international law.

Europe and the INSTEX mechanism

A critical discussion revolved around the role of the 'E3' (France, Germany, and the UK) and European Union in this respect, and particularly the plans to create a financial instrument (INSTEX). Participants presented three debates or 'camps' within Iran: first, that the EU has political will to deliver on its commitments in the JCPOA but has little or no capacity to deliver; second, that both political will and capacity exist but time is needed to implement the INSTEX and deliver on the EU rhetorical commitments; third, that there is capacity but in fact there is no political will to challenge US policy. Increasingly, Iranians have coalesced to this latter position, viewing the EU-US relationship as a 'good cop – bad cop' scenario, in which the EU has drawn out the INSTEX implementation process in complicit support of US economic warfare policy.

One participant summed up bluntly that the EU has done little of concrete value in one year, and if, as expressed by EU Foreign Policy Chief Mogherini, the JCPOA is a security instrument for the EU as well as the Middle East, then it must be invested in. Even if INSTEX were to become immediately operational it was deemed 'useless' as there is no money in it. The Iranian understanding of the INSTEX is that a significant inflow of cash into INSTEX will enable them to purchase the humanitarian goods and raw materials needed, based upon the sale and future delivery of oil which will be kept by Iran in reserve. On their side, Iran has created a reciprocal financial channel, the 'Special Trade and Finance Institute' (STFI), and technical expert consultations with the EU have continued.

Iranians were clear that they are working hard to implement all necessary conditions, such that Europeans will not be able to place the blame upon Iran for any failure. Frustration with EU inaction was widespread and, furthermore, many Iranian participants felt that there was no longer trust towards the Europeans.

On the one hand, some Iranians believed that the US threat of secondary sanctions against European business were in fact hollow: applying and actually implementing sanctions upon these big companies (particularly in oil) was not realistic and they should be willing to trade with Iran without fear of US reprisal. On the other hand, EU countries could quite readily buy oil from Iran by either pre-purchasing through INSTEX or giving credit based on future delivery. A proposal by a European participant with the goal of encouraging such negotiations was that the EU should open an office in Tehran to facilitate diplomacy on both economic and other issues. The baseline position of Iran was that the minimum they expect is to sell their oil, rather than to demand that big business return. Indeed, it was pointed out that if Iran cannot sell its oil then it would logically be against other regional countries using the Strait of Hormuz to sell their oil. Overall, many of those participating believed that the US policy of 'zero oil' exports for Iran is only causing regional tension and instability, beyond the severe hardship for the Iranian economy and the Iranian people.

An end to 'strategic patience'

In this climate, it was made clear that the approach of Iran in the past year in order to keep the deal alive had to change. This shift was also presented as a 'national consensus' decision, from the Tehran elite up to the Supreme Leader. The announced steps to firstly lift the cap on the volume of stockpiled enriched uranium and secondly to increase the level of uranium enrichment above the 3.67% level were viewed as serious, significant, and yet easily reversible, 'within a matter of hours'. A third step has not yet been decided upon within the Iranian bureaucracy: it was indicated that it could relate to the two remaining key provisions of the JCPOA, either lifting the cap on the number of centrifuges or modifying the extent of current research & development activities; equally under consideration would be smaller, incremental steps with respect to enrichment levels and the types of centrifuges deployed. Overall, many Iranians are confident that the measures taken are still in accordance with the JCPOA's provisions on the 'Dispute Resolution Mechanism': following the triggering of article 36, seeking remedy through the JCPOA Joint Commission, they are now acting under article 37, by which 'Iran has stated that if sanctions are reinstated in whole or in part, Iran will treat that as grounds to cease performing its commitments under the JCPOA in whole or in part'.

Beyond hoping that the Europeans will implement and finance INSTEX, as well as modify it to allow not just humanitarian aid but trade as well, discussion touched upon prospects for Iran and the US to engage in some kind of dialogue or even negotiation. It was immediately pointed out that President Trump's central demand of 'no nuclear weapons' was categorically responded to by Iran's Supreme Leader in his meeting with Japanese President Abe in June 2018, and thus this 'precondition' is already present. Iranian participants also reiterated what they see as a permanent commitment not to acquire nuclear weapons based upon the 2003 Fatwa of Ayatollah Khamenei, asking the international participants why this is not viewed as credible in the West. Furthermore, the threat of multiple preconditions was not viewed as a credible basis for initiating a dialogue. One participant conveyed that at the outset of the JCPOA negotiations the EU had tried to include discussions over the regional situation and the ballistic missile programme of Iran but that the US was not prepared to include these because it would mean opening the whole sanctions regime against Iran, rather than limiting the scope of the deal to nuclear-related sanctions only.

Fundamentally, a central impediment to any future dialogue is the current sanctions regime: Iran has stated that it cannot negotiate with 'a knife to the throat' and, with no clearly articulated US policy of what the sanctions will achieve, there appears an impasse. The central message from Iranians was that if progress was going to be made in recommencing dialogue with the US, the nuclear-related sanctions must be lifted. Here, the EU was seen as having the most significant role: it must take action itself with respect to trade with Iran, as well as potentially enabling Russia and China to become involved in INSTEX; and equally in engaging the US in talks to reduce tensions and restart diplomacy. Naturally, it was accepted that a key challenge for the EU is that the US represents its main political and commercial partner, and going against the grain of widespread anti-Iran attitude in Washington is not an easy course of action.

Without significant changes by the US and the EU, the regional situation was viewed as becoming more negatively impacted, while Iran would also continue on its path to scale back its nuclear-related commitments under the JCPOA. Iranian participants relayed plainly that the purpose of the official policy is not to destroy the JCPOA but to save it – many were of the opinion this is a grave moment and may be the last chance to keep it in place. It was felt that the gradual withdrawal trajectory will make clear to the world that Iran has credible and serious options, including withdrawal from the NPT, and will not simply give way to US demands. Yet many Iranians were clear that following one positive step from the EU and US, Iran could reciprocate with a positive step of their own, encouraging a spiral of goodwill.

Regional politics and non-proliferation norms

Discussion also reflected on the regional and international context of the JCPOA: a central understanding within Iran was that the nuclear deal is not only about Iran but reflects the evolving global political landscape. Increasingly, Iran has not only shared strategic interests with Russia and China – and needs them both for economic, political and military support – but as non-aligned states they share a vision of countering US hegemony in the world, seen for example as promoting a de-dollarization of the world economy as part of a new international order. Nevertheless, it was made clear that none of the three countries see an axis or alliance developing, but rather strategic partnerships and co-operation, considering their quite divergent views on some key issues. One international participant stated that China views Iran as a regional power and a 'stabilizing force' in the Middle East. It was suggested that the original turn toward negotiating the JCPOA with Iran under President Obama was a recognition of China's growing influence in Iran and the region more widely. In particular, China's Belt and Road Initiative will not only lock in large levels of economic co-operation across many sectors but, with a planned investment of up to 30 nuclear reactors along the Silk Road, will bring an added non-proliferation challenge to the region.

One participant strongly felt the need to sensitize European and American audiences to proliferation problems occurring on the Arabian Peninsula which threaten to undermine the global nuclear order. It was pointed out that external support of the Saudi nuclear programme is in contrast to the achievement of the JCPOA. For example, Saudi Arabia has not accepted the IAEA Additional Protocol (or even signed the Comprehensive Nuclear-Test-Ban Treaty — CTBT) and is openly hostile towards constraints including inspections and monitoring; Iranians were clear that both the JCPOA and any future possible deal would certainly involve the IAEA performing such tasks. One Iranian participant asserted that Saudi Arabia has the right to develop a civilian nuclear programme but that they must strike a balance on inspections and monitoring in line with global legal obligations. It was noted that, ultimately, all countries must understand that the development of a civilian nuclear programme without a serious system of international control will always create ambiguity with respect to possible military dimensions.

One clear avenue presented for de-escalation of the situation was the Nuclear Weapons-Free Zone (and WMD-Free Zone) proposal, a long-standing initiative supported by Iran in the UN. It was perceived that 'Arab League frustration' led to the transfer of the idea of a regional conference away from the NPT and now under the auspices of the UN General Assembly, with the conference planned to take place in November 2019. While Iranian officials welcomed the conference, there remained wider scepticism of how useful it will prove without Israeli participation. In this vein, it was noted that Israel remains the only regional state to possess nuclear weapons and that this greatly affects the balance of power in the region. As expressed by one Iranian participant, the only guarantee of peace and security is the total elimination of nuclear weapons. The upcoming 2020 Review Conference was viewed as being precariously affected by all of these developments. One participant cautioned that, ultimately, any Iranian withdrawal from the NPT would lead to a Middle East arms race and the potential unravelling of the NPT itself, and every effort from Iran and international partners must be made to avoid such a scenario.

The Middle East continues to be characterised by conflict and war, and it was observed that many actors both inside and outside of the region have 'blood on their hands'. The wars in Syria, Yemen, and Iraq, as well as the conflicts in Afghanistan and the Palestine-Israel problem, have all seriously affected Middle Eastern populations, bringing unbearable suffering, economic costs, and flows of refugees. Participants observed that the rise of extremist ideologies represents the greatest threat not only to the region but to the world, and that all countries have an interest in actions that can define and analyse the problems more clearly rather than pursuing short-term, self-interested policies. For example, European states refusing to allow the return and trial of their own nationals who fought for Daesh exacerbates an anti-Muslim perception. In this respect, one participant felt that oppressed, occupied, or persecuted Muslim communities would continue to be fertile ground for recruitment of disillusioned youth by terrorist groups inspired by Wahabi ideology. It was said that stability in the region must begin with security for all, the promotion of mutual understanding between governments and their populations, and a decreasing reliance upon external arms and military support.

The irony was felt that the JCPOA represents the only example where diplomacy has toned down conflict and provided some success in the region. An effort should be made to establish a 'regional dialogue initiative' that would facilitate reduced aggression and promote regional security and mutual understanding. It was pointed out that the 'non-aggression agreement' proposal of Foreign Minister Zarif to the Persian Gulf neighbours has not been responded to. All Iranians in the meeting expressed support for such a forum that could help in the elimination of conflict and war in the region, and this is a task that, within its limited capabilities, Pugwash could try to help.

At this present time, there is an urgent need to lower rhetoric across the board and to seek out confidence and security-building measures that decrease regional tension. As part of this, it was felt that Iranian narratives and arguments concerning the nuclear programme as well as the region must be presented to other audiences, particularly European and American, in order to promote understanding and a clearer image of Iran's interests and positions. The dangers of the regional situation spiralling and escalating out of control not only pose serious problems across the Middle East but will also impact Europe and the nuclear non-proliferation regime.

www.pugwash.org

Joint Comprehensive Plan of Action

Vienna, 14 July 2015

PREFACE

The E3/EU+3 (China, France, Germany, the Russian Federation, the United Kingdom and the United States, with the High Representative of the European Union for Foreign Affairs and Security Policy) and the Islamic Republic of Iran welcome this historic Joint Comprehensive Plan of Action (JCPOA), which will ensure that Iran's nuclear programme will be exclusively peaceful, and mark a fundamental shift in their approach to this issue. They anticipate that full implementation of this JCPOA will positively contribute to regional and international peace and security. Iran reaffirms that under no circumstances will Iran ever seek, develop or acquire any nuclear weapons.

Iran envisions that this JCPOA will allow it to move forward with an exclusively peaceful, indigenous nuclear programme, in line with scientific and economic considerations, in accordance with the JCPOA, and with a view to building confidence and encouraging international cooperation. In this context, the initial mutually determined limitations described in this JCPOA will be followed by a gradual evolution, at a reasonable pace, of Iran's peaceful nuclear programme, including its enrichment activities, to a commercial programme for exclusively peaceful purposes, consistent with international non-proliferation norms.

The E3/EU+3 envision that the implementation of this JCPOA will progressively allow them to gain confidence in the exclusively peaceful nature of Iran's programme. The JCPOA reflects mutually determined parameters, consistent with practical needs, with agreed limits on the scope of Iran's nuclear programme, including enrichment activities and R&D. The JCPOA addresses the E3/EU+3's concerns, including through comprehensive measures providing for transparency and verification.

The JCPOA will produce the comprehensive lifting of all UN Security Council sanctions as well as multilateral and national sanctions related to Iran's nuclear programme, including steps on access in areas of trade, technology, finance, and energy.

Iran Alert

*Bertrand Russell
Peace Foundation*

In the face of ratcheting tensions, provocations and threats, efforts continue to buttress the Joint Comprehensive Plan of Action (JCPOA) agreed with Iran.

A meeting of the Joint Commission of the JCPOA took place in Vienna on 28 June 2019. The Joint Commission was chaired on behalf of the EU High Representative Federica Mogherini by European External Action Service Secretary General Helga Schmid and was attended by China, France, Germany, Russia, United Kingdom and Iran.

The Russell Foundation with others wrote to those attending the meeting of the Joint Commission, either directly or through their respective embassies, urging the parties to continue their vital work despite the US violating the agreement by withdrawing.

We reproduce *Iran Alert*, the letter sent to the Joint Commission, on the following pages along with a response from Denis Chaibi, Head of the Iran Task Force, on behalf of European External Aaction Service Secretary General Helga Schmid.

Founding President: the Earl Russell, OM, FRS (1872-1970)

The Bertrand Russell Peace Foundation Ltd.

Recipients:
Federica Mogherini
(High Representative of the European Union for Foreign Affairs)
Helga Schmid (Secretary General, European Union External Action)
Ambassador Liu Xiaoming
(Ambassador of the People's Republic of China to the UK)
Ambassador Alexander Vladimirovich Yakovenko
(Ambassador of the Russian Federation to the UK)
Ambassador Hamid Ba'idinejad
(Ambassador of the Islamic Republic of Iran to the UK)
Jean-Yves Le Drian (French Minister of Europe and Foreign Affairs)
Heiko Maas (German Federal Minister for Foreign Affairs)
Jeremy Hunt MP (Secretary of State for Foreign and Commonwealth Affairs, UK)

IRAN ALERT

25th June 2019

Your Excellency,

The Russell Foundation, in common with others, is deeply concerned about the increasing risk of war involving the United States and Iran. A build-up of military forces threatens not only the direct combatants but also the fragile peace of the wider region and the lives of numerous civilians. By repudiating the agreement with Iran in 2018, the United States has violated the carefully constructed deal to ensure Iran remains free of nuclear weapons, notwithstanding their presence elsewhere in the region. Iran was in full compliance with the agreement, as confirmed by successive International Atomic Energy Association inspections, at the time the US withdrew. Such destructive conduct risks proliferation of nuclear weapons and their delivery systems.

The European Union with others rightly seeks to maintain the international agreement with Iran. The Joint Comprehensive Plan of Action (JCPOA), agreed in Vienna in July 2015, seeks to 'ensure that Iran's nuclear programme will be exclusively peaceful ... Iran reaffirms that under no circumstances will Iran ever seek, develop or acquire any nuclear weapons'.

The architects of the plan (China, France, Germany, Iran, Russian Federation, United Kingdom, United States with the High Representative of the European Union) anticipated that 'full implementation of this JCPOA will positively contribute to regional and international peace and security'.

The E3/EU+3 envisaged that implementation of the Plan 'will progressively allow them to gain confidence in the exclusively peaceful nature of Iran's programme'. The Plan limits the scope of Iran's nuclear programme, including enrichment activities and research and development. It addresses the E3/EU+3's concerns, including through comprehensive measures providing for transparency and verification.

Over an extended period, it is envisaged the Plan will 'produce the comprehensive lifting of all UN Security Council sanctions as well as multilateral and national sanctions related to Iran's nuclear programme, including steps on access in areas of trade, technology, finance and energy'.

The withdrawal of the United States did not remove the necessity for the JCPOA approach. We urge the other seven parties to the agreement to continue their vital efforts to make it work.

Yours sincerely,

Ken Fleet   Tony Simpson   Tom Unterrainer
Bertrand Russell Peace Foundation

Caroline Lucas MP, UK
Catherine Rowett MEP, UK
Commander Robert Green RN (Ret'd), New Zealand
Commander Robert Forsyth RN (Ret'd), UK
Bruce Kent, CND Vice-President, UK
Joseph Gerson, Campaign for Peace, Disarmament and Common Security, USA
John Hallam, People for Nuclear Disarmament, Australia
Brian Jones, CND Cymru, Wales
Marguerite Doyle Papadopoulou, Greece
Professor Andreas Bieler, UK
Ian Hewitt, UK
David Browning, UK

Response from the European External Action Service

Dear Mr Fleet,
Dear Mr Simpson,
Dear Mr Unterrainer,

The EEAS Secretary General, Ms Schmid, read with attention your recent letter regarding the US withdrawal from the JCPOA and the proliferation risks of nuclear weapons. Ms Schmid asked me to reply on her behalf.

As you pointed it out, the EU seeks to maintain the international agreement (JCPOA) with Iran, as it seeks to ensure that Iran's nuclear programme will be exclusively peaceful.

This has been confirmed by the Foreign Affairs Ministers of the EU, including in the text they adopted on 4 February 2019.

In this regard, you will have seen that the EU reiterated the need for Iran to continue to implement all of its commitments, and to continue to cooperate fully and in a timely manner with the IAEA.

The European Union also welcomes and fully supports the work undertaken by the IAEA in monitoring Iran's implementation of the JCPOA. The EU welcomes Iran's commitment never to seek, develop or acquire any nuclear weapons.

The EU also recognised that the lifting of sanctions constitutes an essential part of the JCPOA and deeply regrets the re-imposition of sanctions by the United States, following the latter's withdrawal from the JCPOA.

In view of the above, your call to the remaining parties to the JCPOA is welcome.

Let me assure you once again that we are continuing our efforts for diplomacy to prevail.

Yours sincerely,
Dennis Chaibi
Head of the Iran Task Force
9 September 2019

A plan for Iran

Tom Unterrainer

In November 2011, the International Atomic Energy Agency (IAEA) issued a new report titled *Implementation of the NPT Safeguards Agreement and relevant provisions of Security Council resolutions in the Islamic Republic of Iran*. The report, details of which were leaked in advance, raised the following claims about Iran's development of nuclear weapons:

> "The information indicates that Iran has carried out the following activities that are relevant to the development of a nuclear explosive device:
> • Efforts, some successful, to procure nuclear related material and dual use equipment and materials by military related individuals and entities …
> • Efforts to develop undeclared pathways for the production of nuclear material …
> • The acquisition of nuclear weapons development information and documentation from a clandestine nuclear supply network …
> • Work on the development of an indigenous design of a nuclear weapon including the testing of components…"

The report includes a twelve-page annex, 'Possible Military Dimensions to Iran's Nuclear Programme'. Section A of the annex, a 'Historical Overview', notes Iran's commitment to end its nuclear weapons programme from 2003 onwards and its subsequent agreements to sign up to additional protocols for inspection and verification. The 'Historical Overview' then claims that:

Tom Unterrainer works for the Bertrand Russell Peace Foundation. This excerpt is from a longer article on Iran.

"The Agency continued to receive additional information from Member States and acquired new information as a result of its own efforts … Between 2007 and 2010, Iran continued to conceal nuclear activities, by not informing the Agency in a timely manner of the decision to construct or to authorize the construction of a new nuclear power plant."

The annex then proceeds to detail a number of claims already outlined in the report.

Responses to the report came thick and fast. The then Israeli Defence Secretary, Ehud Barak, told Israeli Radio that "We are probably at the last opportunity for co-ordinated, international, lethal sanctions that will force Iran to stop". Israeli Foreign Minister Avigdor Lieberman called for "crippling sanctions" and warned that lack of action would amount to accepting a nuclear armed Iran. Meanwhile, calls for military action grew in the US political establishment.

Anver Cohen, an expert on Israel's nuclear weapons programme, told *The Guardian* that "I think it's 70%-80% bluff that we are planning to attack … Ultimately this is a fight over the Israeli nuclear monopoly in the region". Cohen's colleague at the Monterey Institute of International Studies, Jeffrey Lewis, commented in the same article that "if you strike the Iranian programme you guarantee they are going to turn around and try to make a bomb".

There was significant pressure both within the US and Israel for pre-emptive military assaults to 'neutralise' the alleged threat of an Iranian weapon. Memories of Israel's attack on Iraq's Osirak reactor in the early '80s lingered in the context of a US Presidential race and domestic issues in Israel.

What prompted the change in tone of IAEA reports which, up to this point, had not made such claims? Where was all the new information and intelligence coming from? How to explain the departure in language deployed in this report as compared to similar reports in the recent past? One possible explanation rests on the fact that a change in personnel had taken place at the top of the IAEA. Mohammed ElBaradei succeeded Hans Blix as Director General of the IAEA on 1 December 1997. He was re-elected to serve another four-year term in 2001. Along with his immediate predecessor, ElBaradei disputed the reasons put forward for the invasion of Iraq, and the US subsequently opposed his re-election for a third term in office. Despite such objections, ElBaradei went on to serve a third term which ended with the election of Japanese ambassador Yukiya Amano in 2009. Whilst ElBaradei went on to play a significant role in the fight for democracy in his native Egypt, Amano's succession was warmly welcomed by the US.

In the avalanche of leaked intelligence and other materials disseminated by WikiLeaks, you will find a cable from the US Embassy in Vienna – which has responsibility for relations with the IAEA – detailing its Ambassador's views of the new Director General:

> "IAEA Director General-designate Yukiya Amano thanked the U.S. for having supported his candidacy and took pains to emphasize his support for U.S. strategic objectives for the Agency. Amano reminded Ambassador on several occasions that he would need to make concessions to the G-77, which correctly required him to be fair-minded and independent, but that he was solidly in the U.S. court on every key strategic decision, from high-level personnel appointments to the handling of Iran's alleged nuclear weapons program."

Amano was widely regarded as the US's 'choice' and it seems that he crafted the workings and documentation produced by the IAEA to 'US standards'.

How close the US's 'hybrid' war/strategy came to sparking a full armed confrontation with Iran can be seen in events at the very end of 2011 and in to 2012. In December 2011, the US Congress passed the *National Defence Authorization Act*, section 1245 of which allows for sanctions on any foreign bank found to be processing transactions from the Iranian Central Bank. The new act also allowed for the freezing of assets owned by Iranian financial institutions. Subsection (e) of this section of the Act, under the heading 'Multilateral Diplomacy Initiative' spells out the aims in full:

> "(e) MULTILATERAL DIPLOMACY INITIATIVE.—
> (1) IN GENERAL.—The President shall—
> (A) carry out an initiative of multilateral diplomacy to persuade countries purchasing oil from Iran—
>> (i) to limit the use by Iran of revenue from purchases of oil to purchases of non-luxury consumers goods from the country purchasing the oil; and
>> (ii) to prohibit purchases by Iran of—
>> (I) military or dual-use technology, including items—
>>> (aa) in the Annex to the Missile Technology Control Regime Guidelines;
>>> (bb) in the Annex on Chemicals to the Convention on the Prohibition of the Development, Production, Stockpiling

and Use of Chemical Weapons and on their Destruction, done at Paris January 13, 1993, and entered into force April 29, 1997 (commonly known as the "Chemical Weapons Convention");
(cc) in Part 1 or 2 of the Nuclear Suppliers Group Guidelines; or
(dd) on a control list of the Wassenaar Arrangement on Export Controls for Conventional Arms and Dual-Use Goods and Technologies; or
(II) any other item that could contribute to Iran's conventional, nuclear, chemical, or biological weapons program; and
(B) conduct outreach to petroleum-producing countries to encourage those countries to increase their output of crude oil to ensure there is a sufficient supply of crude oil from countries other than Iran and to minimize any impact on the price of oil resulting from the imposition of sanctions under this section."

Concerns about Iranian plans to develop nuclear weapons and upgrade chemical weapons capabilities are contained in this section. However, subsections A(i) and B seem most clearly to indicate a consolidation and strengthening of existing sanctions aimed at crippling the Iranian economy and punishing the Iranian people, whilst curbing Iran's ability to deploy "conventional" defence measures. How many more signals could the US give to Iran that a military attack was imminent? In January 2012, the following month, the European Union banned member states from importing Iranian oil.

If Iran was truly intent on building a nuclear weapons capability, as the US and its allies insisted – and as the IAEA now seemed to suggest – would this not have been a point at which the country concluded that 'nuclear deterrence' was essential? If Iran was the regional aggressor, commanded by unpredictable fanatics, of the type conjured for public consumption by a generation of pundits, politicians, strategists and the like, would now not be the time for it to adopt a militarily aggressive stance in response to ratcheting tensions? When the US Navy aircraft carrier, the *USS John C. Stennis*, navigated the Strait of Hormuz in early January 2012, did the Iranians meet aggressive posture with an aggressive posture of their own? What in fact happened was that Iran agreed to host a meeting with the IAEA, marking the start of negotiations leading to what became the Joint Comprehensive Plan of Action, or the 'Iran Deal'. Talks between Iran, the five permanent members of the UN Security Council

(P5: China, France, Russia, UK and US) plus Germany (P5+1) progressed through April to July and were described as "positive" by those involved.

In September, Israeli Prime Minister Benjamin Netanyahu addressed the United Nations General Assembly. He took the rostrum to draw a "red line" for Iran's nuclear programme. Given the progress made during the April-July talks, the US drew down on rhetoric threatening military action. President Obama had clashed with the Israeli government over just how urgent military intervention was. Netanyahu, brandishing a 'cartoon' bomb, told the General Assembly that Iran was 90% of the way towards having enough weapons-grade uranium for a bomb:

"I ask you, given this record of Iranian aggression without nuclear weapons, just imagine Iranian aggression with nuclear weapons. Imagine their long range missiles tipped with nuclear warheads, their terror networks armed with atomic bombs …

There are those who believe that a nuclear-armed Iran can be deterred like the Soviet Union. That's a very dangerous assumption. Militant Jihadists behave very differently from secular Marxists. There were no Soviet suicide bombers. Yet Iran produces hordes of them.

Deterrence worked with the Soviets, because every time the Soviets faced a choice between their ideology and their survival, they chose their survival. But deterrence may not work with the Iranians once they get nuclear weapons …

I speak about it now because the hour is getting late, very late. I speak about it now because the Iranian nuclear calendar doesn't take time out for anyone or for anything. I speak about it now because when it comes to the survival of my country, it's not only my right to speak; it's my duty to speak. And I believe that this is the duty of every responsible leader who wants to preserve world peace.

For nearly a decade, the international community has tried to stop the Iranian nuclear program with diplomacy. That hasn't worked. Iran uses diplomatic negotiations as a means to buy time to advance its nuclear program. For over seven years, the international community has tried sanctions with Iran. Under the leadership of President Obama, the international community has passed some of the strongest sanctions to date.

I want to thank the governments represented here that have joined in this effort. It's had an effect. Oil exports have been curbed and the Iranian economy has been hit hard. It's had an effect on the economy, but we must face the truth. Sanctions have not stopped Iran's nuclear program either. According to the International Atomic Energy Agency, during the last year alone, Iran has doubled the number of centrifuges in its underground nuclear facility in Qom.

At this late hour, there is only one way to peacefully prevent Iran from getting atomic bombs. That's by placing a clear red line on Iran's nuclear weapons program."

If the Iranians had indeed progressed 90% of the way towards the enrichment level he cited, Netanyahu wasn't stopping to ask why in any serious fashion. His warning that deterrence – or the prospect of mutually assured destruction – will not work against Iran is an articulation of the well-worn claim that Iranian leaders are singularly irrational. Netanyahu did not explicitly state that Israel would launch military assaults on Iranian nuclear facilities, but the implication was clear.

The UN General Assembly coincided with campaigning for the 2012 Presidential Elections. President Obama was under considerable pressure for not yet having delivered on his promise of a deal with Iran and was subjected to sharp criticism from his Republican opponents. The Republican nominee, Mitt Romney, claimed that Obama was "being too tough with Israel and not tough enough with Iran" following the President's speech to the General Assembly and his refusal to meet with Netanyahu.

Despite the threats, ongoing sanctions and ample room for tensions to boil over into military confrontation, talks between the P5+1 and Iran continued. Obama secured a second term as President and new talks opened in February 2013, only to stall in April. The reason? Iran was preparing for its own elections. Mahmoud Ahmadinejad, widely considered to be a conservative 'hardliner' – including in Iran – was replaced by Hassan Rouhani, a more 'centrist' politician. Upon his election in June 2013, Rouhani called for the resumption of nuclear talks. These talks commenced in September, and in the same month the President of the United States of America telephoned the President of Iran: the first such phone call or discussion since 1979. Rouhani's speech to the 2013 United Nations General Assembly was welcomed by the Obama Administration. The speech is worth quoting extensively:

> "Our world today is replete with fear and hope; fear of war and hostile regional and global relations; fear of deadly confrontation ... fear of poverty and destructive discrimination ... Alongside these fears, however, there are new hopes; the hope of universal acceptance by the people and the elite all across the globe of 'yes to peace and no to war'...
>
> The recent elections in Iran represent a clear, living example of the wise choice of hope, rationality and moderation by the great people of Iran ...
>
> The current critical period of transition in international relations is replete

with dangers, albeit with unique opportunities. Any miscalculation of one's position, and of course, of others, will bear historic damages; a mistake by one actor will have negative impact on all others. Vulnerability is now a global and indivisible phenomenon.

At this sensitive juncture in the history of global relations, the age of zero-sum games is over …

Coercive economic and military policies and practices geared to the maintenance and preservation of old superiorities and dominations have been pursued in a conceptual mindset that negates peace, security, human dignity, and exalted human ideals … Yet another reflection of the same cognitive model is the persistence of Cold War mentality and bi-polar division of the world into 'superior us' and 'inferior others' …

In this context, the strategic violence, which is manifested in the efforts to deprive regional players from their natural domain of action, containment policies, regime change from outside, and the efforts towards redrawing of political borders and frontiers, is extremely dangerous and provocative.

The prevalent international political discourse depicts a civilized center surrounded by un-civilized peripheries. In this picture, the relation between the centre of world power and the peripheries is hegemonic. The discourse assigning the North the centre stage and relegating the South to the periphery has led to the establishment of a monologue at the level of international relations …

This propagandistic discourse has assumed dangerous proportions through portrayal and inculcation of presumed imaginary threats. One such imaginary threat is the so-called 'Iranian threat' – which has been employed as an excuse to justify a long catalogue of crimes and catastrophic practices over the past three decades … Let me say this in all sincerity before this august world assembly, that based on irrefutable evidence, those who harp on the so-called threat of Iran are either a threat against international peace and security themselves or promote such a threat."

Rouhani than moves on to directly address the question of Iran's nuclear programme:

"Iran and other actors should pursue two common objectives as two mutually inseparable parts of a political solution for the nuclear dossier of Iran.
    1 – Iran's nuclear program – and for that matter, that of all other countries – must pursue exclusively peaceful purposes. I declare here, openly and unambiguously, that, notwithstanding the positions of others, this had been, and will always be, the objective of the Islamic Republic

of Iran. Nuclear weapons and other weapons of mass destruction have no place in Iran's security and defence doctrine, and contradict our fundamental religious and ethical convictions. Our national interests make it imperative that we remove any and all reasonable concerns about Iran's nuclear program.

2 – The second objective, that is, acceptance of and respect for the implementation of the right to enrichment insider Iran and enjoyment of other related nuclear rights, provides the only path towards achieving the first objective. Nuclear knowledge in Iran has been domesticated now and the nuclear technology, inclusive of enrichment, has already reached industrial scale. It is, therefore, an illusion, and extremely unrealistic, to presume that the peaceful nature of the nuclear program of Iran could be ensured through impeding the program via illegitimate pressures.

In this context, the Islamic Republic of Iran, insisting on the implementation of its rights and the imperative of international respect and cooperation in this exercise, is prepared to engage immediately in time-bound and result-oriented talks to build mutual confidence and removal of mutual uncertainties with full transparency."

Rouhani's words speak for themselves and, in the context of more than two decades of tension – not to mention the recent ratcheting of sanctions and threats – struck a remarkably defiant tone. Why, at this point, did Iran finally agree to negotiations? Had the threats and sanctions – allegedly targeted against Iranian elites – worked? A surface reading of events certainly points in that direction. But if Iran had actually been working towards nuclear weapons and was '90% of the way' to creating them, why not stall until the job was done? Was the threat of pre-emptive strikes from Israel or elsewhere the deciding factor? Perhaps, but any limited attack on Iran would have merely delayed rather than eliminated the enrichment programme.

Could it be the case that Iran agreed to nuclear negotiations for the simple reasons that it had no nuclear weapons programme and that its approach to foreign affairs is relatively rational?

Postscript: IAEA Director General Amano died on 22 July 2019.

Chemical Weapons – who to believe?

Helena Cobban

The Organization for the Prohibition of Chemical Weapons, with its 193 Member States, is charged with the vital job of implementing the Chemical Weapons Convention. This complex task is fraught with challenges, as highlighted by recent events in Syria. Helena Cobban probes the controversy around deadly attacks in Douma, close to Damascus, in 2018. The author is a Senior Fellow at the Center for International Policy in Washington DC and chief executive of Just World Books and the non-profit Just World Educational (Justworldeducational.org).

In May 2019, a network of UK-based academics challenged allegations – which the Organization for the Prohibition of Chemical Weapons (OPCW) officially corroborated on March 1 – that the Syrian government used chemical weapons against civilians in the outer Damascus suburb of Douma in April 2018. The challenge came in the form of a 15-page assessment, apparently prepared by a team of OPCW engineering experts, that seriously critiqued a fundamental conclusion of the March report. An unknown party leaked this assessment to the UK-based network, the Working Group on Syria, Propaganda and Media. OPCW staff members have indirectly confirmed the authenticity of the assessment.

The main conclusions of the 15-page assessment seem very serious. But its diplomatic and political impact are no less serious. It threatens to bring the still-young OPCW to its biggest political crisis since 2002, when President George W. Bush and his allies unceremoniously ousted its first director-general, José Bustani, for reportedly wanting to deploy OPCW inspectors to Iraq, which could have complicated the lead-up to the invasion the Bush team was planning. (See *Spokesman* 75)

The leaked engineering assessment raises grave questions about the integrity of the OPCW's supposedly apolitical, purely technical internal processes and throws significant doubt on the OPCW accusation that the Syrian government was responsible for several earlier chemical weapons incidents. Douma was, after all, the only site the OPCW's own inspectors were able to visit and inspect. For all the other incidents, the organization had to rely on reports produced by strongly pro-rebel organizations like the so-called 'White Helmets' or Al Jazeera. These reports spread speedily via various web platforms and prompted President Trump and his British and French allies to launch a barrage of 105 cruise missiles against Syrian government scientific facilities on 14 April 2018. Luckily, that act of unauthorized international aggression did not lead to any wider eruption of hostilities.

On 9 April, Syrian government forces quickly retook the locations in Douma where chemical weapons were allegedly used. Syria has been a full member of the OPCW since 2013. On 10 April 2018, it asked the OPCW to 'urgently' send a Fact-Finding Mission (FFM) to Douma to investigate and verify what happened there. On 12 April, an advance team from the FFM arrived in an unnamed 'neighbouring country'. The US-led bombing occurred on the morning of 14 April. Later that day, some members of the FFM apparently arrived in Damascus. Over the month that followed, they were able to interview 13 witnesses and receive environmental and biomedical samples from Douma.

Because of continuing security concerns in Douma, the FFM was unable to deploy any of its team members there for a further week. But between 21 April and 1 May, FFM teams were able to inspect three key facilities in Douma: a hospital that had earlier been a White Helmets outpost and two residential buildings a short distance away, which were tagged in the OPCW report as 'Location 2' and 'Location 4'.

Here are the uncontroversial facts about the Douma incident. While the area was still under the control of the Jaysh al-Islam rebels, some 43 people in the area died ghastly and much-photographed deaths from the effects of a chemical agent believed to have been chlorine, which also wounded an additional number of people. The first photos and videos of the non-fatal casualties were taken (according to their metadata) in the early afternoon of April 7. The first images of dead casualties – many of them in Location 2 – were taken around 10:30 that evening.

By noon of 8 April, electronic images showed, at Location 2, a partly damaged long yellow cylinder thought to contain some chlorine, that was shown lying on the building's reinforced concrete roof, with one end hanging over a hole punched through the roof by an object of similar cross-section. Images from Location 4, meanwhile, showed a similar yellow cylinder, less damaged and still apparently full of chlorine, lying in a top-floor room in whose reinforced concrete ceiling an oval, similarly shaped hole had been punched. This cylinder was not under the hole but off to one side of it, incongruously positioned on a flimsy-looking double bed.

The difference of judgment between the 'final' report on the incident

Gas cylinder in Douma

that the OPCW issued on 1 March and the 'engineering assessment' leaked in May 2019 centred on the provenance of these two cylinders. How had they got to where they were photographed on 8 April and where they were later inspected by the Fact Finding Mission?

By the time the Fact Finding Mission arrived in Douma, the bodies had been long buried. The FFM did not exhume them. In its report, it stated that it was 'not currently possible to precisely link the cause of the signs and symptoms [displayed by the casualties] to a specific chemical'. It stated that no organophosphorous nerve agents (such as sarin) were detected in any of the bio-medical or environmental samples it took, but the deadly chemical could have been 'reactive chlorine' of the kind contained in the two cylinders. The report stated that 'the structural damage to the rebar-reinforced concrete terrace at Location 2 was caused by an impacting object with a geometrically symmetric shape and sufficient kinetic energy to cause the observed damage...' Regarding the cylinder found at Location 4, it stated that, 'The studies ... indicated that, after passing through the ceiling and impacting the floor at lower speed, the cylinder continued an altered trajectory, until reaching the position in which it was found.' That is, the report stated that both cylinders had been delivered to their final, much photographed resting-places by being dropped onto the roof (at Location 2) or through the roof (Location 4.) The report did not specifically assign blame, but the only party using aircraft during the Douma battle that could have dropped the cylinders was the

Syrian army and perhaps their Russian allies.

The leaked engineering assessment punched a hole right through that conclusion. It is dated 27 February 2019 – just two days before the Fact Finding Mission's final report was released. It includes several in-depth studies, including some based on simulations, of what the concrete roofs and their rebar would have looked like if they were impacted or pierced by the cylinders, as well as the damage the cylinders should have registered as result of those impacts. It concluded:

> '[T]he FFM engineering sub-team cannot be certain that the cylinders at either location arrived there as a result of being dropped from an aircraft ... In summary, observations at the scene of the two locations, together with subsequent analysis, suggest that there is a higher probability that both cylinders were manually placed at those two locations rather than being delivered from aircraft.'

If the cylinders were put into their final positions by hand and they were photographed there while Jaysh al-Islam was still in control of the area, then suspicion would of course fall on Jaysh al-Islam – not just for putting the cylinders into position but also for staging the whole incident in a way to lay blame on the Syrian government. Jaysh al-Islam would also likely bear some responsibility for the 43 gruesome deaths recorded in the many photos and videos taken during those two days and circulated so widely at the time.

The leaked engineering assessment contains eight pages of closely argued analysis, a list of appendices, and six pages of technical drawings. The end of the analysis bears the typed sign-off of a senior inspector who has been with the OPCW ever since it started getting staffed up in 1997-98. Each page is headed 'UNCLASSIFIED – OPCW Sensitive / Do not circulate'. The first page is headed 'DRAFT FOR INTERNAL REVIEW' and bears a handwritten annotation: 'Final version – for comments (by hand to TM [Team Members] only.'

The OPCW's formal report contains a 'Mission Timeline' which records that 'consultations with engineering experts' lasted for much of October and November of last year and that 'reception of engineering studies' occupied much of December. Thus, considerable discussion between the engineering team and the FFM's leadership probably took place during those months.

After the engineering assessment was leaked, the OPCW first tried to claim that the document had no standing in the organization. Then, in an email to British journalist Peter Hitchens, it stated, 'the OPCW Technical Secretariat is conducting an internal investigation about *the unauthorised release of the document in question*' – a formulation that seems to concede its authenticity.

Questions about this very disturbing matter have been asked in the British Parliament. Officials in some non-Western states that are OPCW members are also reportedly demanding more information. In the United States, no members of Congress have yet raised this issue. But the Syrian rebels and their supporters have offered recent warnings of possible new chemical attacks in beleaguered Idlib. And on 21 May 2019, a State Department spokeswoman said that the Syrian government 'might be renewing its use of chemical weapons' in that region and warned that any use of such weapons would lead the United States and its allies to 'respond quickly and appropriately'.

Surely, all those who remember how unfounded allegations about Weapons of Mass Destruction were used to catapult the military into the invasion of Iraq should be very wary of that ruse being pulled again.

I remember the hopes that so many of us had, back in the mid-1990s, when scores of countries worked together to negotiate the treaty that established the Organization for the Prohibition of Chemical Weapons. This was the first time that most of the world's nations came together to ban an entire class of horrendous weapons and to establish a body (the OPCW) that could aid and monitor this process. In 2002, President Bush used his power on the world scene in a quite unacceptable way to bully the OPCW. It's important to make sure that the power of the warmongers is not used once again to subvert the OPCW's integrity, a development that could now, as in 2002-03, pave the way for a terrible war.

Update: On 13 June 2019, OPCW Director-General Fernando Arias released the text of a briefing he had given on this matter to the States Parties to the OPCW two weeks earlier. Arias did not utter the name of the long-time OPCW staff member whose name was on the leaked version of the dissident engineering report. But he confirmed that report's author was an OPCW staff member who was 'a liaison officer at our Command Post Office in Damascus,' and 'As such… he was tasked with temporarily assisting the FFM with information collection at some sites in Douma'.

Arias said that because the staff member's report had 'pointed at possible attribution' of the Douma attack, it fell outside the purview of the Fact Finding Mission and therefore received no mention in the FFM's report. However, he said, that on his advice the staff member had submitted it to the separate Investigation and Identification Team working on the Douma incident, which has yet to start work. He stated that three external experts (also un-named) had conducted the analyses of the ballistics/physics of the cylinders' provenance whose conclusions were included in the FFM's 1 March report.

The conclusions of the dissident engineering report have meanwhile been endorsed by Professor Theodore Postol, a distinguished professor emeritus of Science, Technology, and International Security at MIT who has advised US presidents on strategic and scientific matters.

With grateful acknowledgements to Lobelog (www.lobelog.com), where this article first appeared.

Australia and the Bomb

Commander Robert Forsyth RN (Ret'd)

Thinking the unthinkable about Australia deploying submarine-based nuclear weapons, an experienced Royal Navy Commander offers some timely reflections. Commander Forsyth served in the Royal Navy from 1957 to 1981. He commanded conventional and nuclear powered attack submarines, was Executive Officer of a Polaris missile equipped submarine, and led the Submarine Commanding Officers' Qualifying Course.

As a former Royal Navy submarine Commanding Officer who also served as second in command of a *Polaris* submarine, I have read with interest that Professor Hugh White's book *How to defend Australia* includes the suggestion that Australia should revisit possessing its own nuclear weapons because it can no longer rely on the USA's ' nuclear umbrella'. I have spent some time post-service researching the justification for the UK decision to acquire, and now sustain, a submarine launched nuclear-armed ballistic missile system, and the negative effect that this has had on our armed services and the Royal Navy in particular. Australian politicians and military strategic thinkers might care to consider some of my conclusions that apply equally to any State thinking of possessing a 'nuclear deterrent' for the first time.

One first has to ask the question: does nuclear deterrence work? Counter to Cold War ideology, and with the benefit of hindsight, it is now quite clear that nuclear weapons have never deterred any aggression against a nuclear-armed state or a state such as Australia under a US extended nuclear deterrence. Some would argue that the 1962 Cuban Missile Crisis was such a time. However, Khrushchev did not back down for fear of being attacked but because he realised, only just in time, that the biggest danger came not from the USA but from losing control of his own or Cuban nuclear-armed forces who might start a nuclear war the USSR did not want. It is also significant that US nuclear weapons were irrelevant in the Vietnam War in which Australia was deeply involved with its largest military commitment since

World War Two.

Furthermore, and more recently, the risk of nuclear war through miscalculation, mistake or malfunction has, if anything, increased. The much respected Royal Institute of International Affairs, Chatham House, in its 2014 report *Too Close for Comfort* documents some 13 separate occasions when the world has come extremely close to this happening. A subsequent example in 2018 involved a false initiation of a nuclear warning alarm in Hawaii at a time when North Korea was threatening a missile attack against US territory. Former UK Ambassador to Moscow in the 1990s Sir Rodric Braithwaite's book *Armageddon and Paranoia: The Nuclear Confrontation* and Daniel Ellsberg's 2017 book *The Doomsday Machine: Confessions of a Nuclear War Planner* provide compelling evidence of the dangers inherent in possessing nuclear weapons.

Despite this, and without any apparent current or probable future existential threat – Trident missiles have been at 'several days' notice to fire' since 1994 – the UK has decided to continue with its 'independent nuclear deterrent' into the 2050s at a cost of what will likely be well over £150 billion. However, for all this enormous expenditure, UK Trident is not independent. In reality the USA – which leases its missiles to the UK from a common US pool, and whose technical design and support for every part of the weapon system to target and launch them is critical – can frustrate the UK from using Trident if it disapproved. Nor would it be averse to the use of military force to do so. A precedent for this was set in 1956 when the US opposed the Anglo-French Suez campaign. The UK Force Commander at the time, General Sir Charles Keightley, said "It was the (military) action of the US which really defeated us attaining our object". So, unlike France, the UK has opted for nuclear dependence on the US.

Only a force of four nuclear-armed ballistic missile equipped nuclear-powered submarines (SSBNs) would be sufficient to maintain one continuously on patrol. In addition, to maintain its independence from the USA, Australia would need to design and manufacture its own missiles, war heads, specialised satellite navigation, targeting and communications systems and acquire nuclear submarine design, build, operation and maintenance skills. As the UK has learned, there would be a heavy political as well as financial cost for all this; and the Royal Australian Navy would have to develop a major new skills base in operating these highly technical systems. Then there is the need for a nuclear-powered attack submarine (SSN) plus at least one surface ship and maritime patrol aircraft to protect the deployed SSBN. Experience shows that at least six SSNs are required to have one always available for this task. Despite the cost saving by heavy reliance on US equipment, support and expertise, keeping one UK SSBN continuously at sea and undetected places huge and growing strains on a now very depleted and imbalanced Royal Navy.

In fact, the cost of maintaining a UK 'deterrent' has led to the hollowing out of the UK's conventional armed forces to the point where we cannot deter, let alone respond effectively to, aggression against the homeland. For example, the RN fighting fleet has been reduced to six destroyers and 13 frigates: alarmingly, the same numbers of ships sunk or damaged respectively during the 1982 Falklands War. There are new frigates on order, but they barely sustain the number of these key workhorses in the Navy's core role of protecting maritime trade and graduated conventional deterrence. Already the RN is struggling to have enough units to escort one of the two super-carriers *HMS Queen Elizabeth* and *Prince of Wales* . How deeply ironic it is that, as we may be about to exit the European Union, we are having to call on their navies to help protect UK oil tankers in the Gulf because we can no longer do this on our own. Admiral Lord Nelson famously wrote "Were I to die at this moment 'want of frigates' would be found stamped on my heart". There are quite a few latter day Royal Navy Admirals expressing similar sentiments.

I would therefore urge Australia, who would be embarking on an independent nuclear deterrent with no nuclear propulsion or missile experience to build on, to take a long hard look at the effect that maintaining our four *Trident* submarines has had on the defence of the UK homeland. Simply put, it has denied our armed services, especially the Royal Navy, the equipment and personnel they need to meet the wide variety of today's actual threats. Our costly 'nuclear deterrent' has degraded our conventional deterrence capability such that a 'last resort' weapon system would too quickly become the only option left, with associated loss of credibility.

The City of Hiroshima

PEACE DECLARATION
August 6, 2019

Around the world today, we see self-centered nationalism in ascendance, tensions heightened by international exclusivity and rivalry, with nuclear disarmament at a standstill. What are we to make of these global phenomena? Having undergone two world wars, our elders pursued an ideal—a world beyond war. They undertook to construct a system of international cooperation. Should we not now recall and, for human survival, strive for that ideal world? I ask this especially of you, the youth who have never known war but will lead the future. For this purpose, I ask you to listen carefully to the *hibakusha* of August 6, 1945.

A woman who was five then has written this poem:

> Little sister with a bowl cut / head spraying blood
> embraced by Mother / turned raging Asura

A youth of 18 saw this: "They were nearly naked, their clothes burned to tatters, but I couldn't tell the men from the women. Hair gone, eyeballs popped out, lips and ears ripped off, skin hanging from faces, bodies covered in blood—and so many." Today he insists, "We must never, ever allow this to happen to any future generation. We are enough." Appeals like these come from survivors who carry deep scars in body and soul. Are they reaching you?

"A single person is small and weak, but if each of us seeks peace, I'm sure we can stop the forces pushing for war." This woman was 15 at the time. Can we allow her faith to end up an empty wish?

Turning to the world, we do see that individuals have little power, but we also see many examples of the combined strength of multitudes achieving their goal. Indian independence is one such example. Mahatma Gandhi, who contributed to that independence through personal pain and suffering, left us these words, "Intolerance is itself a form of violence and an obstacle to the growth of a true democratic spirit." To confront our current circumstances and achieve a peaceful, sustainable world, we must transcend differences of status or opinion and strive together in a spirit of tolerance toward our ideal. To accomplish this, coming generations must never dismiss the atomic bombings and the war as mere events of the past. It is vital that they internalize the progress the *hibakusha* and others have made toward a peaceful world, then drive steadfastly forward.

World leaders must move forward with them, advancing civil society's ideal. This is why I urge them to visit the atomic-bombed cities, listen to the *hibakusha*, and tour the Peace Memorial Museum and the National Peace Memorial Hall to face what actually happened in the lives of individual victims and their loved ones. I want our current leaders to remember their courageous predecessors: when nuclear superpowers, the US and USSR, were engaged in a tense, escalating nuclear arms race, their leaders manifested reason and turned to dialogue to seek disarmament.

This city, along with the nearly 7,800 member cities of Mayors for Peace, is spreading the Spirit of Hiroshima throughout civil society to create an environment supportive of leaders taking action for nuclear abolition. We want leaders around the world to pursue negotiations in good faith on nuclear disarmament, as mandated by Article VI of the Nuclear Non-Proliferation Treaty, and respond to the yearning of civil society for entry into force of the Treaty on the Prohibition of Nuclear Weapons (TPNW), a milestone on the road to a nuclear-weapon-free world.

I call on the government of the only country to experience a nuclear weapon in war to accede to the *hibakusha's* request that the TPNW be signed and ratified. I urge Japan's leaders to manifest the pacifism of the Japanese Constitution by displaying leadership in taking the next step toward a world free from nuclear weapons. Furthermore, I demand policies that expand the "black rain areas" and improve assistance to the *hibakusha*, whose average age exceeds 82, as well as the many others whose minds, bodies and daily lives are still plagued by suffering due to the harmful effects of radiation.

Today, at this Peace Memorial Ceremony commemorating 74 years since the atomic bombing, we offer our heartfelt consolation to the souls of the atomic bomb victims and, in concert with the city of Nagasaki and kindred spirits around the world, we pledge to make every effort to achieve the total elimination of nuclear weapons and beyond that, a world of genuine, lasting peace.

MATSUI Kazumi
Mayor
The City of Hiroshima

Чорнобиль

Chernobyl

Zhores Medvedev

On 8 August 2019, a deadly nuclear explosion took place in northern Russia in the vicinity of the Nenoksa weapons testing range. At least five people are said to have died. Subsequently, a Russian state weather agency confirmed release into the atmosphere of strontium, barium and other radioactive isotopes, indicating that a nuclear reactor was involved in the explosion.

Zhores Medvedev died in 2018, before this recent explosion. Back in 2011, he charted a trail of nuclear disasters from Kyshtym in the Cheliabinsk region of Russia, to Chernobyl near Pripyat in Ukraine, and to Fukushima in Japan. Dr Medvedev's warnings then continue to ring true. They were contained in his new preface to the Spokesman edition of his book, The Legacy of Chernobyl, *first published in 1990.*

Photos: Lesley Thacker

On 3 February 1987, during a lecture trip to Japan, I was invited to meet five members of the Japan Atomic Industrial Forum Inc. They wanted to discuss my book, *Nuclear Disaster in the Urals,* which described the consequences of the Kyshtym disaster, an explosion at a nuclear waste site in the Soviet Union in 1957.

The book, published in New York in 1979 and translated into Japanese in 1982, was then still the only published description of this accident. The Kyshtym disaster was not yet included in a list of nuclear accidents prepared by the International Atomic Energy Agency (IAEA). Top of this list, recorded at a top-of-the-scale 7 in severity, was Chernobyl, Three Mile Island was scale 5, and the fire at Windscale in England, in 1957, was scale 3. (The International Nuclear Event Scale was revised several times, subsequently, and the fire at Windscale is now reckoned to be scale 5.)

In 1987, I had already started to study the available information on Chernobyl because I was not satisfied with the Soviet Report to the IAEA, which blamed mainly the power station personnel for gross operational errors. My Japanese hosts were not interested in too many details. 'We do not find Chernobyl relevant to Japan,' one of them told me. 'Such accidents can never happen here.'

Nuclear disaster in the Urals

'Kyshtym', a small industrial town in the Urals, was the code name for correspondence among officials about this accident, which actually happened about 60 km east of Kyshtym in a larger but secret town, the first Soviet military nuclear centre, which was in Cheliabinsk region. It was not marked on maps, although the population was nearly 50,000. For scientists who lived there the address was 'Post Box 40, Cheliabinsk'. The first Soviet plutonium-producing reactor was built there in 1948. In 1957, there were three plutonium-producing reactors and a reprocessing plant known as 'Mayak', which extracted plutonium from spent nuclear fuel. Liquid waste after plutonium extraction was transferred to a storage facility built in 1953 about 10 km east of the town. Before 1953 the waste was dumped into the nearest lake, Karachay, and the Techa River. (Lake Karachay is now the largest storage place of nuclear waste in the world.) The underground storage consisted of many steel tanks, each 250 cubic metres in size. These tanks were mounted on a concrete base and covered by a concrete lid. Cooling by water was necessary because the concentrated liquid nuclear waste is hot and can boil dry. In the United States, at this time, boiling was prevented by diluting with water the waste from plutonium production, so it had to be kept in much larger tanks.

Reprocessing involves dissolving the spent fuel in nitric acid, so the waste contains nitrates and acetates, which can be explosive in a dry state. It also produces radiolytic hydrogen, which can accumulate under the lid. (American storage tanks are not covered.) The cooling system in one of the tanks failed and it lost water. Waste started to boil and became too concentrated. On 29 September 1957, a spark ignited the hydrogen, which in turn detonated nitrates, so that a tank containing about 100 tons of waste exploded. The blast was equivalent to about 100 tons of TNT. This is a reconstruction, made later. Many details of this event were never disclosed. It is still not known what happened to the whole storage facility.

Most of the radioactivity, 20 to 50 million curies, was dispersed around the storage facility, but about 2 million curies of isotopes of caesium and strontium in aerosol form rose up to two kilometres in the air and distributed over a large area in a north-easterly direction. The radioactive cloud covered an area of 23,000 sq.km. of agricultural land. There were 217 villages and settlements here, with a population of 270,000. Early snow and the absence of equipment and personnel complicated the measurement of contamination. During the next two years, about 10,000 villagers from an area of about 1,000 sq.km. were resettled. Nineteen villages were destroyed by fire to prevent people returning. Agricultural production was stopped over a larger area.

I learnt about this disaster in 1958, when my friend V. M. Klechkovsky, then chairman of the department of agrochemistry of the Moscow Agricultural Academy, was appointed head of the programme for rehabilitation of contaminated agricultural land. Some of my close friends from student years moved to the area to work. The risks were high, but salaries were also very high. Their work, however, was classified as 'top secret'.

In November 1976, already living and working in London, I briefly mentioned an explosion of the nuclear waste site in the Urals in a British magazine, *New Scientist*. Two days later, the Chairman of the United Kingdom Atomic Energy Authority, Sir John Hill, in an interview with the Press Association, published in many countries, described my story as 'pure fiction, rubbish and figment of imagination'. American scientists made similar comments. An explosion of nuclear waste was considered impossible. However, in 1977, I published in *New Scientist* more details about the ecological effect of this accident. Then the discussion moved to a different level. In 1978, I was invited to several US National Laboratories (Argonne, Oak Ridge, Brookhaven and Los Alamos). Everywhere I was told that such a serious accident could not happen without American scientists finding out about it.

In Los Alamos in November 1978, Edward Teller, the creator of the American hydrogen bomb, questioned me very aggressively for nearly three hours. He accused me of a deliberate attempt to frighten the western public about the dangers of nuclear power, which was being widely promoted at the time. The report of the Los Alamos National Laboratory, published in 1982 (D. V. Soran, D.V. Stillman, *An Analysis of the Alleged Kyshtym Disaster*) attempted to explain this radioactive contamination by a nuclear weapon test.

The disaster was partially declassified in 1989. The local population started to demand the same financial compensation and medical attention as the victims of Chernobyl. Only in 1990, when the Soviet authorities formally acknowledged this accident, was 'The Kyshtym Disaster' included in the list of nuclear accidents by the International Atomic Energy Agency. It was given severity scale 6, between Three Mile Island and Chernobyl. In 1990, as a participant of the Kurchatov Institute of Atomic Energy Conference on Kyshtym, I had an opportunity to visit the site. I also visited the local cemetery to see the graves of two of my friends who had died from leukaemia.

The secrets of Chernobyl

The Chernobyl disaster has been comprehensively studied, but many aspects are not well known.

The Chernobyl reactors are Soviet designed and built, a source of pride at the time. RBMK-1000 is a graphite moderated reactor using slightly enriched uranium (2% U-235). It is a boiling water reactor with two loops feeding steam directly to the turbines. The use of a graphite moderator allows a reduction of reactor pressure, but also makes the reactor core very large, 7m high and about 12m in diameter. That is why no containment vessel was made. Raising or lowering 211 control rods regulated the reactivity. One drawback of the RBMK reactor, well known to the designers and to the IAEA, was the 'positive void coefficient', when an increase in steam bubbles (voids) causes an increase in core reactivity. The shutdown procedure was dangerously slow at about 10 seconds.

The State Commission created by the government to study the accident prepared a detailed Report in August 1986, which was presented to the IAEA and discussed there at a special international conference. The accident was blamed on incredible errors and the incompetence of the operating personnel. The director of the Chernobyl plant, chief engineer, his deputy and several operators of Reactor 4 were arrested, tried by the Supreme Court of the USSR, and sentenced to ten years in prison for criminal neglect in operation of a potentially explosive system. Research into the causes of the explosion continued. The main puzzle was that the explosion happened a few seconds after an operator, L.Toptunov, pressed the red 'panic button' for emergency shutdown, and the control rods started to move down. Neither Toptunov, nor his supervisor who gave the order, survived to stand trial.

In January 1988, the Soviet journal *Atomnaja Energia* published a paper by the physicist E. Adamov and others on the first phase of the Chernobyl accident.[1] They concluded that the real cause of the explosion was a design fault of the control rods which were inserted into the reactor core to slow down the fission reaction. To gain some extra power the lower part of each control rod was graphite, and beneath the rods channels were filled with water. The upper part of the rod was made of boron carbide, which absorbs neutrons. With this design, during the first seconds after the 'panic button' was pressed, 170 rods started to move down at once, slowed by having to displace water, not absorbing neutrons, but instead producing a surge of reactivity in the lower part of the reactor core, resulting in the explosion due to the increase in criticality and reactivity. The operators did not know about this possibility, and it was the first time in Toptunov's short life that he had used the emergency button. The conclusion of the paper in *Atomnaja Energia* was that the dramatic increase in reactivity (nearly 100 fold) was a direct result of the design error.

Figure: Scheme of the position of graphite ends of the control rods of the RBMK-1000 reactor

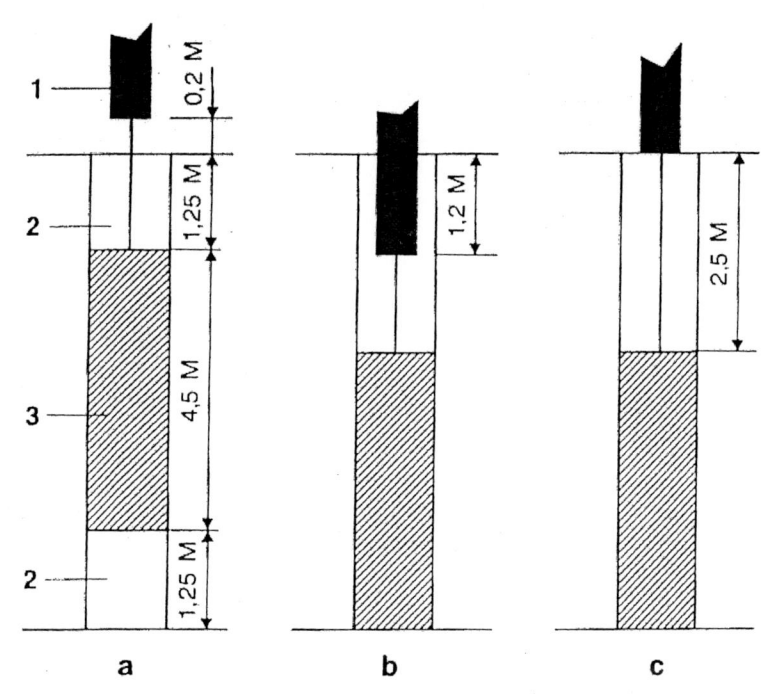

1. Boron parts of the control rods position in working reactor
2. Connection between rod and graphite end supplement
3. Graphite end
   a. Before Chernobyl accident
   b. After Chernobyl accident in other RBMK reactors
   c. After redesign in 1987

(From Adamov et al)

The Commission did not report this fault to the International Atomic Energy Agency in August 1986. But it was known to the designers of the RBMK model. All the other 15 RBMK reactors in the USSR[2] were instructed to continue operating, but with the control rods descended down into the core by 25% of their length. This reduced generation of electricity to 70% of projected power. Billions of kilowatts of electricity were lost. Later the control rods were redesigned (see Figure).

The official acknowledgement of the design fault of the RBMK reactors was slow. A special amendment to the 1986 Government Report was sent to the IAEA in Vienna only in 1991. It made clear that the RBMK-1000 reactor did not correspond to safety norms and had some potentially dangerous features. 'The operators did not violate any rules and their actions did not contribute to the development of the accident ...' This conclusion appeared in the IAEA papers only in 1993, when the USSR had already disappeared. The general press in the Russian Federation, and in Ukraine and Belarus, reported nothing about the rehabilitation of the management and personnel of the Chernobyl plant.

The Chernobyl disaster contributed heavily to the economic, political and social crisis that developed into the collapse of the Soviet Union. Between 1987 and 1991 nearly 60 nuclear reactors of different types, including thermal and experimental, were either closed down or frozen in the construction or project stage. The programme of thermal nuclear stations to heat some cities (Gorky, Odessa, Voronezh, Rostov-Don) was cancelled, although they had already been built and tested. The Armenian nuclear power station was stopped after the earthquake in 1988. A shortage of electric power resulted in the cancellation of many industrial projects. Because Ukraine and Belorussia were mainly affected by radioactive fallout from Chernobyl, local nationalist movements, which were embryonic before 1986, became major political forces. When I was in Ukraine in 1991 for the International Conference on the Ecological and Medical Consequences of the Chernobyl Accident, there was a demonstration in Kiev on 26 April with placards that said 'Stop the Radiation Genocide of the Ukrainian People'.

The other three Chernobyl reactors continued to work for many years. The last of them was shut down in 2000 under pressure from the European Union. (The EU promised compensation which never materialised.) Work on cooling the spent fuel storages and the nuclear reactor cores, and servicing and sealing the damaged reactor, continues today with thousands of workers in round-the-clock shifts. The whole site is expected to be dismantled by 2065, after two periods of decay half-lives of caesium-137 and strontium-90. However, the dismantling cannot be carried out without a new, much larger protective structure, which has to cover the original sarcophagus and the whole site. This structure is designed to prevent the release of radioactive debris and dust from the destroyed reactor into the environment. The technology for this dismantling will be developed later. The new project, which is known as the 'New Safe Confinement', with an estimated cost of $600 million, is expected to last 100 years or more. Because Ukraine is unable to finance the project, the United Nations has been collecting donations since 2006. Nearly 50 governments have promised to contribute. But the French company, which was awarded the contract in 2007, still performs only preparatory work. It may take a decade before the actual dismantling of the destroyed reactor will start.

Fukushima: The improbable can happen

The first nuclear reactor for the Fukushima I plant was designed in the early 1960s, ordered in 1966, and put into operation in 1971 for the Tokyo Electric Power Company (TEPCO) by General Electric. It was modest in terms of power; a 460 MW boiling water reactor (BWR). The second reactor of the same type was more powerful (784 MW), and the last (the sixth reactor), which came into operation in 1979, was 1100 MW. The design was expected to withstand seismic events of magnitude 7,5. This was the force of the California earthquake of 1952. The San Francisco earthquake of 1906 was 7,8. The Great Tokyo Earthquake of 1923 was magnitude 8,3. The earthquake on 11 March 2011 was magnitude 9.

The Fukushima I nuclear accident is now considered the second largest after Chernobyl. But it is still developing, and might yet take the lead in the IAEA list of nuclear accidents. It is much more complex because it involves several reactors and the spent fuel storage tanks, with about 25 times more radioactivity than there was in the Chernobyl reactor. The picture of the accident grows darker and darker almost daily: partial meltdowns in reactors 1, 2 and 3; hydrogen explosions which destroyed the upper parts of buildings housing the reactors; damage to the containment inside reactor 2; fires and leaks. The amount of radioactivity released into the environment has already reached the Chernobyl level. However, in Chernobyl the release was gases and aerosol into the air. In Japan, there are mostly radioactive solutions which contaminate soil and sea. (In Japan, there is also much more plutonium.)

Igor Ostretsov, a nuclear engineer of Soviet pressurised water reactor (PWR) models, whom I consulted, wrote that the location of the emergency power generators so close to the sea and at sea level, just facing the great tectonic fracture, was a serious mistake. He also considers unfortunate and unsafe the location of very heavy spent fuel storage tanks filled with water in the same building above the reactor. Such a location made it easier to load the fuel rods from the reactor into the storage pool, but it also made 'suspended' storage tanks very vulnerable to any earthquake.

The earthquake damaged these tanks, causing them to leak. Their location made it difficult to refill them with cooling water. Helicopters and fire engines were used out of desperation.

Another design fault identified by Ostretsov was the absence of a ventilation system for radiolytic and zirconium-steam reaction produced hydrogen gas. This resulted in accumulation of the gas in the reactor building, and caused explosions which destroyed the building and many critical systems, particularly the cooling loops. The use of seawater was another desperate measure, as the water evaporates, leaving salt, which further damages the fuel rods in the core and in storage pools.

The boiling water reactor (BWR) system has one more problem. The same water, which functions as a neutron moderator and is part of the fission control, is also feeding steam directly to the turbines without an intervening heat exchanger. This purified and deionised water is pumped to the bottom of the fuel channels and boils, producing steam used to drive the turbines. This water accumulates fission radionuclides.

Heavily contaminated water, particularly with iodine-131 and caesium-137, is the main problem. Reactors do not produce carbon dioxide, which is an advantage. But they produce an enormous amount of heat. Working reactors therefore consume a huge amount of cooling water; 21,000 tons per hour in Fukushima I-1, 33,300 tons per hour in Fukushima I-3, and 48,300 tons per hour in Fukushima I-6. Even after shutdown, residual heat from accumulated radionuclides constitutes up to five per cent of project power (depending on the fuel cycle), enough to cause meltdown. Partial meltdowns were reported at Fukushima after the emergency shutdown. Thus, several thousand tons of water per hour are still needed to cool the residual heat of the cores and the spent fuel in storage. With the circulating systems damaged, this water has to be dumped in the sea. There is no project provision to store this amount of radioactive water. Temporary storage was possible only for the reduction of iodine-135 (half-life 6,7 hours) and iodine-131 (half-life 8 days). The iodine isotopes were produced in working reactors. (Nearly 80 million curies of radioactive iodine were released into the air in Chernobyl.)

Now, nearly three months after the Japan earthquake, the danger from iodine has diminished. The main problems are strontium-90, caesium-137, plutonium and a few more long-lived radionuclides. The danger of new meltdowns is not yet over. The main problem for years to come will be managing more than 500 tons of spent fuel in the reactors and in storage pools, more than 4 tons of which is plutonium. The cooling systems of the reactors and spent fuel tanks were found beyond repair and the current methods of cooling continue to wash out the radioactivity into the environment. The project to dismantle the whole nuclear plant with its six reactors might take many years.

The legacy, the lessons, the future

It is clear that all the stages of nuclear generation of electricity and all models of reactor design are susceptible to malfunction and human error. Human errors were made not only in the design, engineering and operation, but also in planning oversights, such as not taking into consideration the possible force of earthquakes and tsunamis. Earthquakes with magnitude 9 are not unprecedented in Asia.

The Three Mile Island accident in 1979, the most frightening meltdown of a pressurized water reactor (PWR), resulted from trivial failures in the non-nuclear secondary system and human errors. Melting of nuclear fuel rods and zirconium-steam reaction, with the release of large amounts of hydrogen gas, developed from residual heat after the reactor was shut down. The zirconium oxidation itself releases a lot of heat. It is self-sustaining, like a fire. Overheating with the generation of hydrogen is also possible in spent fuel storage tanks if some of the rods are exposed due to the loss of cooling water.

There have been many reactor accidents below severity level 4 which were very close to becoming disasters: the Leningrad Atomic Electro Station (AES) RBMK-1000 reactor in 1975; a fire at the Armenian AES in 1982; and several reactor accidents on nuclear submarines and icebreakers which were not reported to the International Atomic Energy Agency. The first Soviet nuclear icebreaker, *Lenin,* built in 1957, suffered partial reactor fuel meltdowns twice, in 1965 and in 1967. Reactors made for ships and submarines are more prone to accidents because they operate at much higher levels of uranium-235 enrichment. Soviet designed naval reactors were fuelled with U-235 enriched to 21-45 per cent. After decommissioning, spent fuel in such reactors contains too high concentrations of radioactive isotopes so that it is more 'hot' and difficult to handle.

Nuclear power is consumed as electricity without the accumulation of carbon dioxide. However, it constantly accumulates spent fuel rods, which generate intense heat and dangerous radiation for years. Fresh spent fuel rods which are removed from any reactor every 12 to 18 months are the most dangerous due to short-lived isotopes, such as iodine-131, and these are kept close to the reactor under intensive cooling. Without water the spent fuel can suffer meltdown. The duration of this danger of 'criticality' depends on the level of enrichment of uranium-235. The quality of cooling water is tightly controlled to prevent the fuel or its cladding from degrading. The use of sea water for cooling nuclear storage pools certainly produces damage, which will complicate the removal of these rods for permanent storage or reprocessing. Spent fuel rods need water cooling for many years. The system also requires removal of radiolytic gases, hydrogen and oxygen.

It is clear now that spent fuel pools as well as reactor cores should be equipped with back-up water circulation systems and separate back-up generators for water circulation. The Three Mile Island accident resulted in nearly one hundred new safety requirements in nuclear power station design and operation. The Fukushima accident will probably generate even more. We might have safer reactors in the future, but they will be more expensive and take more time to build. The nuclear generation of electricity will for many years, if not decades, continue to use old and immature technology. In 2011, there are 178 nuclear reactors, out of a total of 444 that are generating electricity worldwide, which are more than 30 years old and obsolete.

Zhores Medvedev, London, May 2011

References
1. Adamov E.A. et al., *Atomnaja Energija* Vol.64, No 1, pp 24-29, 1988.
2. Information about reactors of different types is taken from *Directory of nuclear power plants in the world 1994,* edited by Haruo Fujii and Atsuyoshi Morishima, Japan Nuclear Energy Information Center Co., Tokyo, Japan

Chernobyl, 2019

Agbogbloshie Blues

Gregory Woods

1

The beauty of this narrow berth
decreases if there's less of it.

2

Unwilling to admit a dearth,
we squander the largesse of it.

3

Perhaps Mankind was set on Earth
to make a swirling cess of it.

4

In which case, Lord, for what it's worth,
we've made a great success of it.

5

Indulging our Creator's mirth,
we wallow in the mess of it.

Note: Agbogbloshie, or ToxiCity, is one of the most polluted places on the planet, one of the West's favoured dumps for electronic items. It is a suburb of Accra, Ghana. As a boy I used to eat fish caught in the estuary there.

Working with Bertie

Ken Coates

In 1997, Ken Coates gave the annual Bertrand Russell Peace Lecture at McMaster University in Canada, which holds the Bertrand Russell Archives. Whilst there, he reflected on his experiences working with Russell during the last years of his long life, from 1965 until 1970, and how the Bertrand Russell Peace Foundation faced the challenge of continuing Russell's work once he was gone.

This discussion is in part reminiscence and in part a current perspective on carrying on Bertrand Russell's work. It concerns the whole remit we had when Bertie died and the experience we subsequently gained in trying to continue some of his projects when he was no longer with us. It also concerns tomorrow and what we're going to do next.

Where to start? The problem is that Russell has a monumental reputation as a philosopher and as a man who, in certain spheres, is the archetype of consistency and intellectual rigour: a person to whom people look for the nearest thing that's available, in an agnostic universe, to some kind of certainty. Of course, it isn't really like that. But it is true that Russell established his crystalline reputation as a thinker and, at the same time, carried out a lifetime of political activity, a large part of which was expressed in the various books he wrote.

The very first book was a political work, a description of German social democracy. A very interesting work, it still stands up. While it served as an introduction to a novel political force, it also had a very important academic significance. In it he laid out, before the Italian political sociologist Roberto Michels had ever been heard of, something very close to the theory that Michels advanced of the 'iron law of oligarchy', which described how power was inexorably centralized within democratic political parties so that 'socialists may triumph' in Michels words, 'but socialism never'. Russell was very concerned to measure the pretensions of the German socialists against the likely consequences of their activity.

From there on he didn't only move straight into the foundations of geometry and other more recondite academic works, but he also continued to molest the political domain with a whole string of works, some of which were absolutely high explosive. During the First World War the various books and tracts which were subsequently published as *Justice in Wartime* had a dramatic impact. He actually went to prison for some of the things he wrote as a pacifist in the later months of that war. And then he went off to Russia and to China, so that the people of the Bertrand Russell Archives at McMaster University are in the process of producing what I hope will be very revealing studies of the background to the published writings of those days: for they were fascinating writings. After that we had a whole series of writings on the problems of political power in Europe, on anarchism and freedom, and on pacifism. And at the very end of his life the writings were about nuclear disarmament, about the balance of global power, about the dreadful events in Vietnam, about the crisis in Cuba; there flowed a whole string of tracts and books. How consistent was all this political output?

It is my belief that there is a very strong degree of consistency, but it is not to be found simply in comparing texts, nor is to be found in the maintenance of an identical political position across contexts. To a superficial observer, you could say that Russell sometimes looks like a weathercock; he points this way, he points that way. When you look at what he said about nuclear weapons, you can find him pointing in this direction this decade round and in the contrary direction in the next. And sometimes you can find him struggling with intractable realities and going to opposite conclusions within a time span of a couple of decades. Now for most people a couple of decades is a devil of a long time, and not so many of us can be found to be completely consistent over such a period of time. But we haven't all published a shelf full of books to record the movement of our opinions for future critics.

I want to talk about some of these problems, but the first consideration has to be this: that political action – even on such broad issues as human survival, on such questions as the nuclear arms race, on general matters of pacifism or the preparation of war – is necessarily a contingent affair, subject to mobility, to fluidity of movement. In public affairs it is not possible, or at least it has not yet been possible for anybody I have ever known, including Russell, to present a book of rules which can be inflexibly followed to produce a desired result, which will always be replicated whenever the prescription is repeated. None of that is possible. What actually happens is that you find yourself dealing with huge social pressures, sometimes volcanic pressures and you find yourself trying to persuade people to act and react when they are most reluctant to do anything at all. In fact, too often people are extremely reluctant to do what perhaps they ought to do and frequently they owe allegiances to others who are even more refractory, intransigent and uncooperative. All of that means that politics is still an art and one in which those of us that tread into it quite normally fail. I don't trust a politician who isn't at least partly ready to admit failure. It is a very difficult thing to produce results that everybody wants in the solid political contexts in which we have to operate.

This was true even in the early days of the formation of the Campaign for Nuclear Disarmament. Originally, Russell confronted nuclear weapons with almost a sense of relief that now, perhaps, war would at last become impossible. This entailed the hope that the possession of nuclear weapons by one power, especially if that power could be persuaded to share and cede control over them to a responsible international body, might mean that the outbreak of war might be effectively inhibited. But the technology of nuclear weapons advanced extremely rapidly and the monopoly of nuclear weapons was broken almost immediately. And then we got the race between the great nuclear powers to perfect thermo-nuclear weapons, followed by the race to create more and more versatile rockets. With the arrival of the H-bomb, Russell took alarm, and he then launched his Pugwash Appeal with numerous Nobel scientists, but jointly sponsored by Albert Einstein, to oppose the hydrogen bomb and to call for the beginnings of what became a global nuclear disarmament movement. By very speedy stages, we arrived in Britain at the formation of a Campaign for Nuclear Disarmament, the enrolment of large numbers of distinguished people, the mobilization of campaigners, demonstrations, efforts to persuade political parties, social organizations and all the rest of it.

Today all of this is presented in a fairly straightforward manner. However, at the time there was a lot of argument about it. Russell's own apparent earlier inconsistencies were highlighted, and no doubt they'll have to be highlighted again when the appropriate volumes in the *Collected Papers* will appear. But the interesting thing is what happened when the political processes in Britain were tested by the spectacular advance of this most successful of Russell's campaigns, for there was a tremendous enthusiasm among young people for the Campaign for Nuclear Disarmament. The cry 'Ban the Bomb' was everywhere. The arguments about the meaning of unilateralism became very powerful. This argument quickly spread into the Labour Party, which was relatively open and a relatively democratic option in Britain, and which was very much influenced by what the young people were doing. Labour MPs found that their children were marching to and from the nuclear weapons manufactory at Aldermaston. I slept on several floors with the sons and daughters of extremely important politicians. The argument, after the march, literally went home with them. And all these distinguished people found themselves debating with their children and, some of them, found themselves actually moving with the tide of youthful opinion.

In a very short time, the Labour Party found itself divided, found itself voting more than once on the issue of whether the policy of Her Majesty's Opposition would henceforth oppose the ownership of nuclear weapons by the UK.

The story was as follows. The leader of the Labour Party was a partisan the Atlantic Alliance, a man of very firm principle. People said he was a rather inflexible man. Certainly, he couldn't accept the argument for unilateral nuclear disarmament and, in the end, he went down to defeat in a vote at the Party conference. After this he made a very famous speech in which he pledged to 'fight and fight and fight again' to save the Party he loved. Well, he didn't exactly save it, but he certainly reversed the commitment to nuclear disarmament.

The easiest way to achieve this reversal was to persuade various important trade union leaders, who in the structure of the British Labour Party, actually dominated the votes. Because the trade unions had block votes, if you had a million members you could cast a million votes. It was very difficult for the individual members to muster something equivalent to that. In the end Mr. Gaitskell and his friends talked to all the trade union leaders and in no time at all they had assembled a reverse majority for keeping the bomb.

Two things happened and they brought Russell into a new position. That is to say, we had a political choice. Young Ralph Schoenman, facing these circumstances in which the political authority had first been persuaded of the justice of Russell's case and then rejected it, thought that this meant that the political processes were silted up beyond challenge and that it was necessary to confront the civil powers in a campaign of civil disobedience. For historical reasons, that was an attractive argument to Russell who had been involved in civil disobedience himself in the period of the First World War and who had certainly had many pacifist friends who had suffered in prison for their refusal to cooperate in that war effort.

So there began a campaign of sit-downs. I was on the first one, which was in Trafalgar Square. We all sat there. And the more intrepid and courageous, or the unluckiest, of us were arrested, borne off by the police, and subsequently sent to prison, initially for short periods of time. Later, as further sit-downs followed, they were sent to prison for longer periods of time and then longer still. Most of Russell's intimate advisors, of whom I was not one at that time, actually faced very considerable repression. They served long months in prison.

My view of this was that it was entirely justifiable for people to register their protests and I had no objection in principle to civil disobedience. The question at issue was what is a sensible strategy for a political movement. And let me put it to you what such a strategy entailed. It entailed taking all the most courageous, all the most dedicated, all the most persistent advocates for your cause and putting them in line to be separated from the rest. Now it always seemed to me that the important thing to do when you're involved in a battle of this kind was to spread your courage as evenly as possible and ensure that all were fired by the same motives. So I had great doubts about a policy which separated people. I didn't think that the Committee of 100, which was the civil disobedience movement, was unjustified or wrong and I didn't regard it as fair to accuse them of splitting. I thought that it was entirely natural that they should be impatient and cross and resistant to the fact that the political process was so deliberately obstructed. But it also seemed to me that we had to deal with the political process and remove the obstructions.

I was approached by a young man called Richard Fletcher who looked into all of this and persuaded me that the victory in the Labour Party for the restoration of nuclear policy was based not on all the trade unions, but a very restricted number, and that one in particular was the key to the question. That was the Engineers' Union. And the Engineers' Union had a long democratic history. Its members were rather radical. They were not all passionate nuclear disarmers, but they were more *pro* nuclear disarmament than they were *contra*. While their national committee had voted repeatedly in favour of nuclear disarmament their leader who held their block vote, which determined their position in party voting, was an establishment man, and over a period of time he had consistently cast the union's vote against nuclear disarmament even though his members had cast their votes in favour of it.

Ergo, we had to see what could be done to democratize the voting within the Engineers' Union. So, we launched a little newspaper. We got together with engineering workers, and we created a campaigning focus, not just about nuclear disarmament but about all the issues that engineering workers were concerned about. To our surprise, we got an enormous degree of support from those people. *Engineering Voice* became quite a popular newspaper and in due course, it discovered a candidate who would run for the presidential elections. Shortly afterwards, he won.

What brought him into office was the most spectacular manipulation of his predecessor who was in the end cornered by his own history of constantly voting against the mandate given to him by his members. His parting shot was to cast the union's block vote on both sides of the question, thus annulling it. He voted against nuclear disarmament and he voted for it, and, of course, we lost the game. But that was the last time. The union elections transferred power to someone who could be trusted not to do that. From then on, the Engineers' Union was led by a man who was, in this respect, a consistent democrat. He would not have cast a vote against his members, even if he deeply disliked what they wanted him to do. This meant that the Labour Party was henceforward a different place. The way was cleared for a long, subsequent development, in which different ideas prevailed. When we formed the European Nuclear Disarmament campaign, some time later, we did it with the total support of the then Labour Party.

Now, I don't claim that this was a superior way to behave than the way Russell himself and Ralph Schoenman and the other young people were moving. It isn't like that. It is a political process. All that sitting down, and although it cost us a lot in terms of the number of years of imprisonment served by good people, none the less raised the profile of the issue, stirred the consciences of those of us who were more reluctant to volunteer for a term in prison – it made sure that all of us were highly motivated and it gave some inspiration to the engineers. You must remember that Bertie himself went to prison. Nehru told Galbraith, 'He is more free than any of us'. He was the most popular prisoner of the decade and they were discussing this in the factories. It was seen as being an important act of defiance, not only on the nuclear question, but on a whole range of issues about which popular discontent was running high.

I think the point is important. At the time, you could have entered the Campaign for Nuclear Disarmament and, undoubtedly, would have encountered a lot of heat and argument about what was the right thing to do. But in the end, all the things that were done contributed to a change in the overall position. As always that is determined by the issues chosen, by the way in which the question of nuclear disarmament was centred. So in the words of the poet, John Donne, he who would seek truth 'about must and about must go'. There is more than one way of pursuing a proper objective. That is my first lesson.

Now there is a second lesson which is also, I think, unavoidable ...

The second point I want to make covers slightly different ground because I want to come back to the story of the Campaign for Nuclear Disarmament in a later period than that in which Russell was happily in the forefront. As the movement for nuclear disarmament continued, we got a series of events culminating in the most horrific confrontation which was the war in Vietnam.

Last week, I had a telephone call from Professor Ray Monk, who is now a very famous biographer of Russell. He's just published the first volume of his study. It is scholarly. It is very well written. It actually gives me the impression that he doesn't like Bertrand Russell very much. But he can be forgiven for not liking someone whom we are very fond of. That happens. Now Professor Monk is busily working away to prepare his Volume II. The other day he drew my attention to a little book called *War Crimes in Vietnam*. Russell was at this time being advised and assisted by some of the young men who volunteered to help him at the time of the sit down protests against the Bomb. In this book Bertrand Russell thanks this group of young men for the inputs that they made into researching and preparing the texts that are included in it. These are the same young men who actually encouraged him into supporting the Committee of 100 in direct action. Chapter 8 of this little work worries Ray Monk very much indeed because it is called 'Peace Through Resistance to US Imperialism', which he thinks is quite contradictory to what he described as Russell's other commitment to peaceful coexistence.

First of all, I don't really accept that dichotomy, although I must say why I do accept that peaceful coexistence in the broad meaning of that term was an engagement which united millions of sensible people and most of the people who were in favour of nuclear disarmament. While Russell did use the words 'peaceful coexistence' from time to time, actually 'peaceful coexistence' wasn't an invention of Russell's by any manner of means. It was a famous slogan of the Russian government, and it betokened their policy for the continuation of peaceful relations, which meant essentially that no government should get in the way of Russian objectives and, in turn, the Russians would not get in the way of Western objectives. Most of the time, most people would agree that such a stand-off was better than a nuclear war, even if they were often very unhappy about the objectives pursued by either side, or both.

This was not an unalloyed recipe for peace. Dastardly things were being done on both sides and the nuclear stand-off could freeze in continuity all the dastardly deeds in the world. If you said 'well we're going to ignore all of that in order to get on with peacefully coexisting', the world could become quite a miserable place for some of the people caught in between the contending powers.

Peace and Justice do not always sit well together. If there were Justice, would there be Peace? It would be nice to know. I will offer you an example of this. When we were trying to carry on the legacy of Bertrand Russell, we ran a tribunal in West Germany on what was called the *Berufsverbot*, which was a kind of McCarthyite law, sacking communists from public offices of responsibility. Which communists got sacked? Not the nice man who was spying in Willy Brandt's office, but usually the postman or the village schoolteacher. German radicals got onto us and we agreed to constitute a tribunal of inquiry. It worked over three sessions and we drew a lot of attention to *Berufsverbot* and I think we made the German government rather ashamed of this. At the end of the day, we received another proposal from Vladimir Dedijer, one of the tribunal's principal spokesmen, and a famous Yugoslav historian, together with a number of others, suggesting that we should go on to conduct a tribunal into the atrocities that had been committed in Russia since the 1917 Revolution and that we should judge all of the human rights violations that had happened in their country.

Now this is precisely where you hit the frontiers. There was a division in the Foundation and Bertie was gone, unfortunately. We had to decide what to do. The majority of us thought that it would be a mistake to run such a tribunal. I do promise you that we were not soft on the atrocities committed in Russia. We had all spent years defending political prisoners, defending victims of a wide variety of different oppressions in Russia. We weren't at all naïve about the extent of breaches of civil liberty and about the astonishingly savage history of Russia in between the wars and during the Second World War. We were familiar with these problems, but the question that we had to face was that this tribunal was proposed as an event to take place in West Germany, precisely at the moment when Willy Brandt had become the Chancellor and was driving full steam ahead with the programme of *Ostpolitik*, which was an attempt, if you like, at peaceful coexistence; an attempt to establish more normal relations between East and West and particularly between East and West Europe. Some of us argued that if we were to run such a tribunal, this would be extremely popular in parts of the press in West Germany, which hated Willy Brandt, and it would be used to prove that Willy Brandt was a communist stooge. While we weren't entirely uncritical of Willy Brandt, who also took responsibility in part for the *Berufsverbot*, we thought that peaceful coexistence had its due claims on us and that such an investigation could happen anywhere, but not in West Germany and not at that time.

Now I'm telling you that tale, which is a digression, because I want to make it clear that I don't think it was at all possible to ignore the claims of 'peaceful coexistence', but I think that there is a permanent tension: what iniquities do you put up with in order to secure the peace? And what iniquities do you feel to be so profound as to demand opposition come what may? And where do you draw the line? And how can you be sure that if you oppose this iniquity you don't actually tilt the scales so that you produce results which run away to produce conflicts that you hadn't anticipated and that you profoundly oppose. Those are the difficulties and they are all political judgements. I defy anybody to show me a rule which will enable me to judge beforehand all those possible outcomes. You have to develop a feel for it. It's a political process. We might have been wrong in the 1970s to reject that call. I don't really believe we were, but this was the kind of problem that was confronting Russell a decade earlier when he was confronted with all the pain of the war in Vietnam. Here was a man who had preached incessantly about the need to prevent a nuclear confrontation, who preached all the time about sensible steps toward nuclear disarmament, who had made it very clear that he well understood that the world could tip over into mutual annihilation. And yet, as Ray Monk says to me, he writes a chapter in this book, which appears to show that the American atrocities in Vietnam are so unbearable, so awful that America has to be defeated. Now that sounds very strange.

My view of this matter is, first of all, that the proof of the pudding is that we have eaten it. The Americans were defeated and the world did not come to an end. And not only were they defeated in Vietnam but, as a result of the defeat in Vietnam, there was a whole series of very important changes in which different colonial movements were able to take power in a variety of countries: Mozambique, Angola, Portuguese-Guinea, a wide sweep of dominoes which the US State Department had warned us about — that if Vietnam fell then there would be dominoes going here and there. The dominoes weren't in South East Asia, as had been foreseen, but they were wherever the authorities were beleaguered. The most important domino was in Europe. It was called Portugal, which, because of the upheaval in the Portuguese colonies, changed government and became, at last, a democratic government after half a century of fascism. I am glad that domino went down. Aren't you? A lot of people in Portugal were glad.

Now that is also a political judgement and don't let's stop there, let's run way in front. One of the people who helped Bertie in preparing his case against the American conduct in Vietnam was an American scholar called Gabriel Kolko, who taught at York University. He wrote some brilliant papers about the origins of the Vietnam conflict and gave, what I think, was perhaps the most important testimony to the War Crimes Tribunal in Stockholm. Kolko has been spending years studying what happened in Vietnam and he is about to publish a book which is absolutely horrifying. It is a book about the evolution of Vietnam. And it is, for those who remember those earlier days, a book which gives us a terrible feeling of anti-climax, of distress, because the evolution in Vietnam has been extremely painful. Kolko makes this completely plain.

This is another datum we have to grasp, which is that the best intentions of people do not necessarily lead to the results they anticipate. It is also true that if you want to look at the history of Vietnam you've got to look at the whole surrounding environment, you've got to look at all the other pressures in a global political system which is devoted to control and to extinction of the kinds of experiments that the Vietnamese wanted to make, and that their western supporters wished to see given the chance to flower. It didn't happen.

What I am saying is that the world is now quite complicated and it was very complicated for Bertie. He didn't have a key that could tell him what was going to happen in the future. He had to respond to what there was. And what there was in Vietnam was an absolutely outrageous and horrific war of repression. It was completely cruel and what he did was to stand against it, in a way which I think was immensely courageous. In standing against it, he inspired a whole generation of young people to oppose it. Now he couldn't get them to oppose it by saying that on the one hand it was this and on the other hand it was that and, on balance, the Americans might be behaving in a way that ought not to be encouraged. He organized the opposition by calling down comminations on the adversary who was, in this case, the American government.

It may sound shocking to say this, but I'm trying to be truthful in terms of my own experience at that time. Remember what happened in the immediate aftermath of this. In the days after this little book was published, you got the bombardment by the US Airforce, not only of Vietnam, but by President Nixon and Henry Kissinger of Cambodia. It was the most horrendous experience. Truly, it was a holocaust. Five miles up in the air, vast bombers rained hundreds of thousands of tons of high explosives on these Cambodian settlements. People were burned alive. A whole generation of young people who, by some miracle or other, survived, orphans usually, came out of the villages into the jungle and were formed into the Khmer Rouge. It is absolutely clear that these people were frequently deracinated by the pain and anguish through which they had lived and they went on to exact an horrendous toll from other Cambodians who were different.

This is not a story which is easily told to show who was right and who was wrong. But I can tell you who is certainly wrong. The architect of that bombardment was absolutely wrong and we gave him the Nobel Peace Prize. Now Bertie could never be accused of condoning that. But Bertie was also a very great man, even though Mr. Monk might have a different opinion, and what he said exercised influence. Most of us can exercise nothing like that degree of influence because we work in our sphere; we do what we can, we have our friends, we have such influence as we have, and we have to join together with others, in order to be able to effect anything whatsoever. So we can't simply follow Russell and do as Russell did. We have to find ways of acting politically.

Now I can move back from this. One of my jobs when I finally joined the Russell team after much resistance was to look after a number of human rights desks. It was so easy when Bertie was alive because we had all these political prisoners, East, West and neutral, and we have their wives, their families and their political supporters calling on us to do things. We would discuss this, draft letters, and Bertie would send off these letters and immediately they connected on the desk of the State or the Prime Minister and immediately the Prime Minister would pick up the phone to the Chief of Prison Administration and say 'have you got this fellow so-and-so? They're all saying that you're torturing him' or 'you're ill-treating him' or 'you're not feeding him properly'. Even if it didn't go any further than that, the diet of our prisoner immediately improved, for you can't have the headman inquiring without all the minions in the prison service trembling. Sometimes it went far beyond that; Bertie secured a number of people's release and he secured commutations of death sentences. The records are all at McMaster University. I think that when they're gone through, you'll find they are quite impressive.

We want to carry on Russell's work, and he's dead. We know all these political prisoners and we're still getting all the letters, because people kept on writing to Bertie as if he were still very much alive for ten years after he'd gone. But now we can't write a letter: I can't just up and say 'please let out Mr So-and-So and stop torturing him, signed Ken Coates'. Who's that? I mean such a letter goes straight in the bin. So what we had to do was to find substitute Berties. But it's quite difficult. We had to go trawling around the great and the good. How many great and good on a prison begging letter amounts to half a Bertie? Well, I can tell you it's a devil of a lot. We used to have to get our petitions signed by twelve or twenty and frequently a hundred distinguished people in order to get less than the result that Bertie got with one letter. We carried on doing it and we carried on with these cases and I was very pleased. In 1982 we got Ben Bella out of house arrest. I'd been campaigning and working with Bertie when they put Ben Bella into prison. Over the whole of that period we rained protests on the Algerian authorities, and in the end we got him out. When he came to London he told us lots of things that were very interesting. One of the things he told us was that he'd been locked up with a copy of a French translation of the first volume of Joseph Needham's wonderful book on *Science and Civilization in China*. So we took him to Joseph Needham and it was a lovely meeting. Bertie would have loved to have been there.

The work could be carried on, but it had to be carried on in totally different circumstances and that is the perhaps most noticeable thing about trying to continue the work of someone like Bertrand Russell who is just not dispensable. He was unique.

But these major conflicts continued. In 1979, the Russians decided that it was time to up the notches a bit and they deployed, or threatened to deploy, SS20 missiles all across Eastern Europe to teach the Americans that they weren't going to be messed about with and they weren't going to be threatened with neutron bombs and all the other paraphernalia which was current at the time. And the Western response to this was to deploy cruise missiles and Pershing II missiles across six countries in a sort of facing arc.

That is when Edward Thompson comes into the story because Edward wrote to me when these decisions were announced and he wrote to the leaders of the Labour Party who were, remember, in favour of nuclear disarmament at this time. He said to them all: let's run a campaign of civil disobedience against the deployment of all these American missiles at Greenham Common [US military base in the south of England]. That's what the peace activists instinctively thought of doing. They had learnt it from Bertie. I got copies of the letters from the Labour leaders, too, because I was very close to them at that time and so I was piggy-in-the-middle. What was clear was that Edward was perfectly justified in thinking that civil disobedience was an appropriate response to this deployment. And goodness me, we got civil disobedience all over Europe soon after. But it was politically not possible to expect the leaders of a constitutional political party, about to contest an election, hoping to form the government, to say 'oh well, we're going to adjourn that for the time being and run some civil disobedience'.

I consulted widely about this with all kinds of friends in and around the peace movement and we decided to put up the suggestion that there should be a new thing: an overall European campaign, East and West, for nuclear disarmament. We wanted to make Europe into a nuclear-free zone. The Russians could keep their weapons and the Americans could and the way to ensure that it wasn't targeted was to withdraw all the nuclear weapons from both sides and send them home to the principal contenders. Edward thought that was a very good idea and he immediately sat down and wrote a very nice draft about it. We debated it and altered it and sent it all over Europe for endorsement. The Labour political leaders also thought it was quite a good idea and they gave their support and convened a press conference in the House of Commons. Very soon we were away and we got many thousands of signatures. And so we got a European campaign for nuclear disarmament.

Because we had had the experience of working with Bertie, I think we were able to avoid some of the pitfalls into which the earlier nuclear disarmament movement fell. We were able to avoid over much worry about whether people were sitting down or signing petitions. If you want to sign petitions, get on with it. That's great. If you feel like starting a peace camp, or doing a spell in prison, well OK, we'll do our best to help you. The question at issue was that people should act in their own way. What we were able to do, which was interesting, now leads me into the third part of what I want to say.

Having got, in England, co-operation from the peace movement, for whom Edward was truly an authentic voice, and the co-operation of a large part of the political movement, because when the Labour Party came with us, the Liberal Party was disposed to help us and quite a number of other smaller parties, the Nationalist parties all rallied round, we found ourselves creating a forum in which these spontaneous peace organizations, other long-standing, non-governmental organizations, and the political parties all began to plan their joint action. In the end, we were able to get a European Convention. It took some doing but we got a congress, first of all in Brussels, of about eight hundred different representatives and, subsequently, in Berlin with several thousand representatives. This was a genuine meeting in which all these spontaneous activisms met with social democracy, with some parts of Christian democracy, with the liberals, with massive involvement from the churches. So we found ourselves working with a genuine movement which, in certain circumstances, could organize a million to demonstrate in each of six different capitals on the same day or on the same weekend. What I learned from this is that there is no Chinese Wall between political representation and voluntary peace activism. There is no Chinese Wall between the different denominations. But what is necessary is to devise projects which can genuinely liberate the enthusiasms and the involvement of all the most generous people in society. Once you've done that you can begin to work towards giving the constituency for change a real chance of prevailing.

Now we've shut the circle because that is where we are at today. To carry on the work of Bertrand Russell isn't a question of following to the letter his different prescriptions. You can find many different prescriptions and some of them you can follow in an ever-diminishing circle, and you know where that will lead you. The question of carrying on Russell's work is seeing the broad architecture of what he was trying to do and, essentially, that was about creating a space not only for human survival, but for self-organization and the development of humane impulses. Russell didn't set out with this architecture in mind. He came to need this architecture as he worked through the different campaigns in which he involved himself.

What did we know, those of us who supported him? I must say, for the record, that my support grew slowly. The first time I met him, I had a serious disagreement with him. Slowly I came to the view that we had to be together and that he was towering over the other political choices available in Britain at that time. Working with Russell changed your view of him. And I can say that all of us who were involved with him in those final years came to love him very deeply indeed. But this wasn't a question of becoming uncritical fans. Learning through each process, helped us to learn for the next one. What I don't know is whether it will help us to learn in time for the ones to come because the worst and most difficult troubles of humanity are coming in the next millennium. I think that they are more difficult than the earlier ones to overcome, but I also think we've got lots of young people who are more clever than their predecessors ever were.

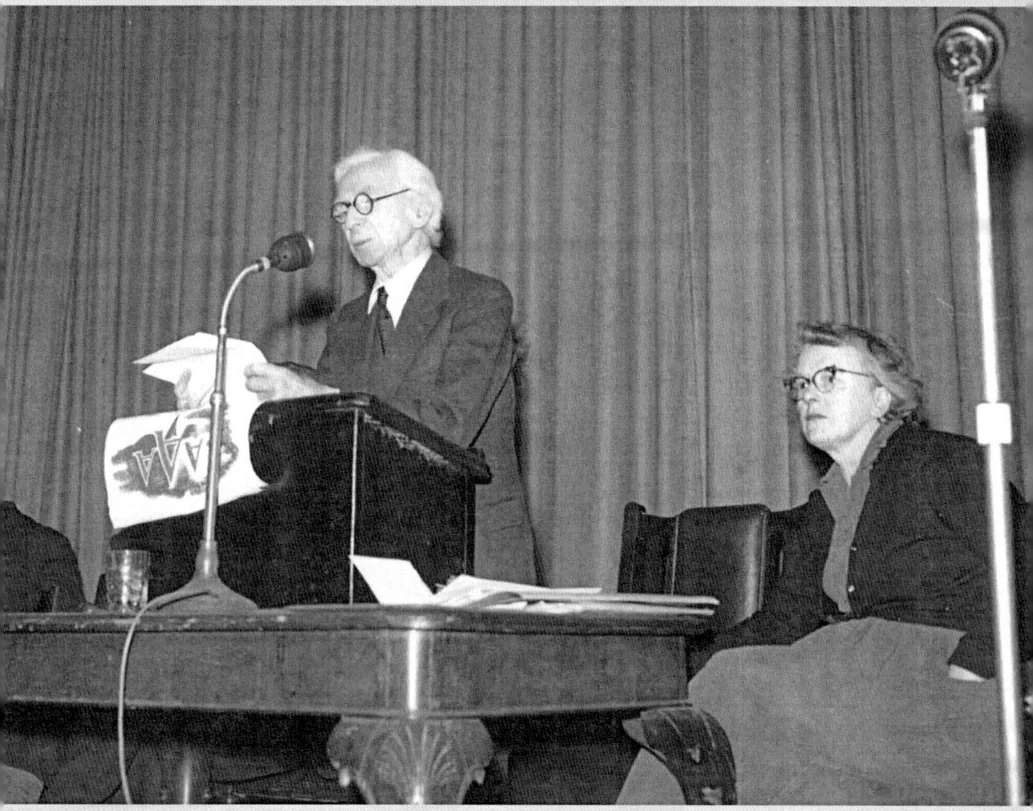

Before CND

Peggy Duff and Ken Blackwell

In February 1971, shortly before the publication of her book, Left, Left, Left *, Peggy Duff was interviewed by Ken Blackwell, Archivist of Bertrand Russell's papers at McMaster University in Canada. McMaster acquired Russell's Archives in 1968. Ken Blackwell catalogued the papers in Britain, including at Russell's home in North Wales, prior to their dispatch to Canada, which has become the global centre for Russell studies. This excerpt is from the opening part of the interview. Explanatory notes have been added in square brackets. Details of Spokesman's new edition of* Left, Left, Left *are at the end.*

◀ *Russell with Peggy Duff*

KB: This is Ken Blackwell interviewing Mrs Peggy Duff, who has been with the British CND [Campaign for Nuclear Disarmament] movement for its entire history and who is now lecturing in North America, touring the campuses, finding out what's going on in the American peace movement. Peggy, you're looking at a book called *Mud Pie: The CND Story* by Herb Greer. What do you think of that book as a history of the CND movement?

PD: It is very hostile and in some cases, so far as I remember, inaccurate.

KB: Has there been a decent history of the CND movement?

PD: Well, the best one is Christopher Driver's.

KB: Yes, we have that one. *The Disarmers*.

PD: That's the best one so far I think. Canon Collins wrote about it a bit in a book called *Faith Under Fire* – or *Fire Under Faith*, I forget which one. Of course, there's my own that's coming out this summer.

KB: Which is called?

PD: *Left, Left, Left*.

KB: And that's to be a history of your involvement in politics?

PD: In a number of campaigns, of which CND is one.

KB: In front of me I have the earliest file of [Bertrand] Russell's, from Russell's involvement with campaigns for nuclear disarmament.

PD: 1955.

KB: Yes, 1955. There are several letters to do with his talk at the end of 1954, called 'Man's Peril from the Hydrogen Bomb'. That started things going for him. He got Einstein to join with him in a big statement in July 1955, there's a scientists conference in August 1955 and a book was published later on that year called *The Bomb: Challenge and Answer* [published] by McAllister.

PD: Of course, that was the period when Britain was agreeing to go ahead with the H-Bomb in the House [of Commons]. Aneurin Bevan opposed it, not because he was totally against nuclear weapons but he was against the first use. Massive Retaliation, in fact.

KB: He was for Massive Retaliation?

PD: No, he was against Massive Retaliation. He believed in a second-strike force: you had to have them as a deterrent. I think he was wrong, but that was his position. But he almost got expelled from the Labour Party because he refused to vote for the party resolution on the H-Bomb. That was '54-'55 and that was when Britain went ahead with building the H-Bomb. Previously, they'd been building the Atom Bomb.

KB: In 1956, not much seems to have happened with Russell except that he was busily organising the first Pugwash Conference in '57.

PD: There was a campaign in Britain called 'The H-Bomb Petition' that was run by Anthony Greenwood, Anthony Wedgwood Benn [Tony Benn], Julius Silverman. It was very inefficiently run by a man named Arthur Carr and it organised a petition and held an Albert Hall meeting which was not very successful. They had about 500 people in the Albert Hall, which looked very bad. But it's interesting that some of the people involved like Tony Wedgwood Benn later were supporting the Labour government keeping of Polaris [missiles] etc. I don't think Russell was involved in that [petition].

KB: No, I don't see any letters from him on that.

PD: After that, apart from Pugwash, there was really nothing until the National Council for the Abolition of Nuclear Weapon Tests started, which grew out of a group in Hampstead.

KB: Did Suez have anything to do with it, or Hungary – both happening in '56.

PD: I think it's possible that people switched interest from the bomb for a period and then the whole thing zoomed up again in '57 partly because of the tests at Christmas Island which, because they were British tests, caused a lot of excitement; partly because there had been a big campaign inside the Labour Party and it was expected that the 1957 conference of the Labour Party might pass a resolution for the unilateral renunciation [of nuclear weapons]. They failed to do it, partly because Aneurin Bevan opposed it. That was the famous split between Aneurin and the Left. That was one of the roots, because it was after the Labour Party failed to pass this resolution that Russell and Priestley and these people started to get together to start some organised resistance. Until then they thought that the Labour Party was going to do it.

KB: In late '57 Russell wrote an open letter to Khrushchev and Eisenhower. Khrushchev replied and [US Secretary of State] Dulles replied. Khrushchev replied again. At this time [former US Ambassador to the Soviet Union, George F.] Kennan had given the Reith Lectures [on 'Russia, the Atom and the West'] and then CND was formed. How did …

PD: Well, it all came from different routes. There was the failure, in early October, of the Labour Party to pass this resolution and particularly the defection of Aneurin Bevan. It was the first time that the Left and Aneurin had split. The tests at Christmas Island went on through all the summer of '57 and the National Council for the Abolition of Nuclear Weapon Tests was the only organisation at that time which was providing any sort of organised resistance. There were a few local committees which set out on their own in places like Oxford and Reading which were operating without any national presence. And then there were the Russell letters to Khrushchev and Eisenhower, and the replies. And Kingsley Martin [editor of *New Statesman* magazine, got involved]. There was a lot of correspondence after that, articles by J.B. Priestley in the *New Statesman*, there were the Reith Lectures by Kennan and, as a result of that, there were two separate things that came together: the National Council decided that it should enlarge its aims to include campaigns against the weapons, not just the tests and at the same time there was this meeting in Kingsley Martin's flat in the Adelphi between Kennan, Russell, Priestley, [Nobel Prize winning physicist Patrick] Blackett and [Stephen] King-Hall, I think, at which it was agreed that some of them – like Blackett – would operate within the Establishment and that a public campaign should be mounted. The two go together. The initiative from Russell, Priestley and Kingsley was to organise a public campaign. I got in touch with them and the thing was merged.

KB: Do you think that Russell ever operated within the Establishment at that time?

PD: Not in the same way that Blackett did.

KB: Was Blackett successful at all?

PD: I think that to a certain extent they succeeded in creating some doubts and some alarm. I think that it's notable that later, by something like 1960, we had at least one General who was publicly opposing nuclear weapons.

KB: Have you read that interesting book by C.P. Snow, *The Corridors of Power*? He talks about an effort to get nuclear disarmament from within the Establishment.

PD: Yes.

KB: In front of me I have what I suppose is your first letter to Russell, 9th September 1957. Do you remember writing it?

PD: Yes, vaguely. That was an appeal for funds.

KB: This is before CND got started.

PD: It was before the Labour Party conference. It wasn't the first time I'd met him. He'd been involved in an earlier campaign I'd organised between 1945 and '49 called 'Save Europe Now', which was concerned with political campaigns against starvation in Europe but in particular for relief of both ex-allies and ex-enemies.

KB: Was that an all-party campaign?

PD: It was a Victor Gollancz campaign.

KB: What part did Russell have in it?

PD: He was one of the sponsors and he used to come to meetings.

KB: Did he speak for the movement?

PD: Yes. We held some public meetings. We raised a lot of money. We got bread rationed in order that there should be more bread for Europe. It was typical of a Gollancz campaign because Gollancz always did things you would never expect him to do. He was Jewish and he organised a campaign for help to Germany after the war. He did the same thing later for Arabs. We organised a campaign in '47 for repatriation of prisoners of war, who were still in Britain and should have been sent home. That was successful. We had a big meeting at Albert Hall, right at the beginning – it must have been about the end of '45 – and I think Russell spoke at that.

KB: Did you meet Russell in those days?

PD: Yes, I met him at meetings. He came to one meeting and I can remember him saying that if it wasn't for the Atom Bomb – because in those days there were just Atom Bombs – in the hands of the United States, that the Russians might be at the Channel Ports within a few weeks. He was very anti-Soviet at that stage.

KB: Yes. In Volume Two of his *Autobiography* he retracts that, he says he was misled.

PD: I think he was misled. He had the courage to admit it.

KB: Did you know Russell on a personal basis?

PD: A bit, yes. A bit.

KB: What was he like? Did he have all his faculties?

PD: He was very much on the ball. He would come to the meetings and, unlike a lot of people, he never said anything unless he had something to say. He was always brief and very incisive. He was always like that, you wrote him a letter and you got a brief reply which gave you everything you wanted.

KB: How was he as a 'committee man', both in those days and later on, in the Campaign.

PD: In the Campaign, he very rarely came to committees. I think this was a mistake. He was presumed to be a 'President' – sort of a 'House of Lords' – and the Executive would meet and he was very rarely invited and very rarely came. He was invited to speak at meetings. He did a lot about the European conference that we tried to hold in the summer of '58 but which was banned in Basel [Switzerland]. He spoke at the subsequent conference held in London the following January 1959. He did one or two things, like when we were banned in Basel he wrote the Swiss Confederation a very rude letter.

KB: What did he say?

PD: He said that it was not surprising that a country that even now refused the vote to women would ban a conference on nuclear weapons. He did everything he was asked. I think one of the tragedies of the subsequent split between the Committee [of 100] and CND was that he would really have been willing to do far more, but wasn't asked to.

KB: That is a pity. I'm just looking through all these folders with Russell's correspondence with you and other people in the Peace Movement. Here's a letter from you saying: 'Dear Lord Russell, Many thanks for speaking at our meeting on Monday'. What meeting do you think that was?

PD: I think it must have been at Central Hall.

KB: 'Most people seem to think it was an historic occasion', you wrote. 'Secondly, I've had a request for an article on nuclear disarmament from the Yearbook of Leeds Trades Council'. Do you remember that book at all? What we're trying to do in these archives is to trace down everything that Russell wrote, and we don't have this book.

PD: The Leeds Trades Council – they should have it.

KB: So I could write to them, then?

PD: Yes.

KB: Oh, I see, and a synopsis of his speech at the Central Hall meeting was used.

PD: Do you have that?

KB: We have that speech and it's just been re-printed in a book called *The Rhetoric of the British Peace Movement*, with some comments which aren't so good. Oh yes, here's another letter from you asking Russell if you can print his speech as a leaflet.

PD: Yes, presumably we did.

KB: The archives don't have that leaflet.

PD: I'll see if we've got it, but I'm not sure.

KB: Here's a letter from the Aldermaston March Committee.

PD: That was the first one. It was a separate *ad-hoc* committee.

KB: And that handled the first Aldermaston March?

PD: Yes.

KB: Which became part of the CND movement after?

PD: Afterwards, CND organised them ...

With grateful acknowledgements to Ken Blackwell for his permission to publish. Transcribed by Tom Unterrainer from the McMaster Digital Archive.

LEFT, LEFT LEFT

A personal account
of six protest campaigns
1945-1965

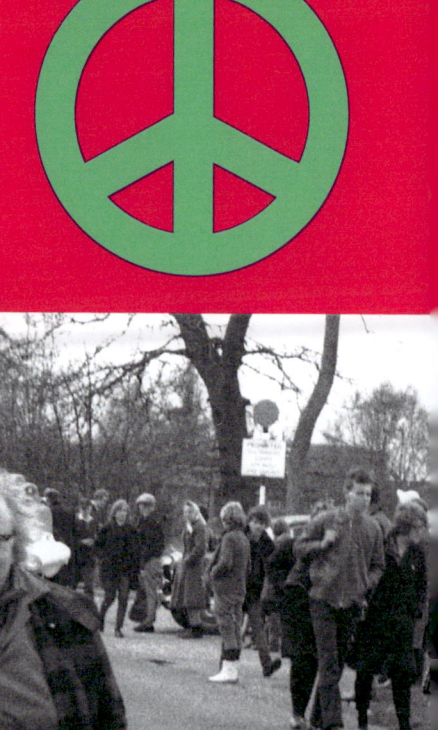

Peggy Duff

"Peggy Duff is one of the unsung heroes of the struggles for peace and justice in the post-World War II period. She was a founder and leading figure in the Campaign for Nuclear Disarmament, which was instrumental in bringing the dire threat of nuclear war to general attention. Among activists, if not the general public, she is widely recognized – by some (like me) virtually revered – for her incredible contributions to the international movement of protest against the US wars in Indochina. Peggy was indefatigable, a highly effective organizer, patient and persistent in bringing together the many complex strands of opposition to US crimes in Indochina, the worst of the post-war era. Only those deeply involved were fully aware of this impressive accomplishment, which alone would easily merit the Nobel Peace Prize. And it was far from her only major achievement. The list ranges from her defence of the rights of prisoners of war in the early post-war years to her courageous role in the thankless struggle for Palestinian rights.

Truly a remarkable person, and speaking personally, a close and deeply valued friend."

Noam Chomsky

2019 Edition, published by **Spokesman Books**
publishing imprint of the
Bertrand Russell Peace Foundation

308 Pages | A5 Paperback

Fully Indexed | 12 Pages of Photographs

ISBN 978 0 85124 8813 | £15.99

available from:
www.spokesmanbooks.com

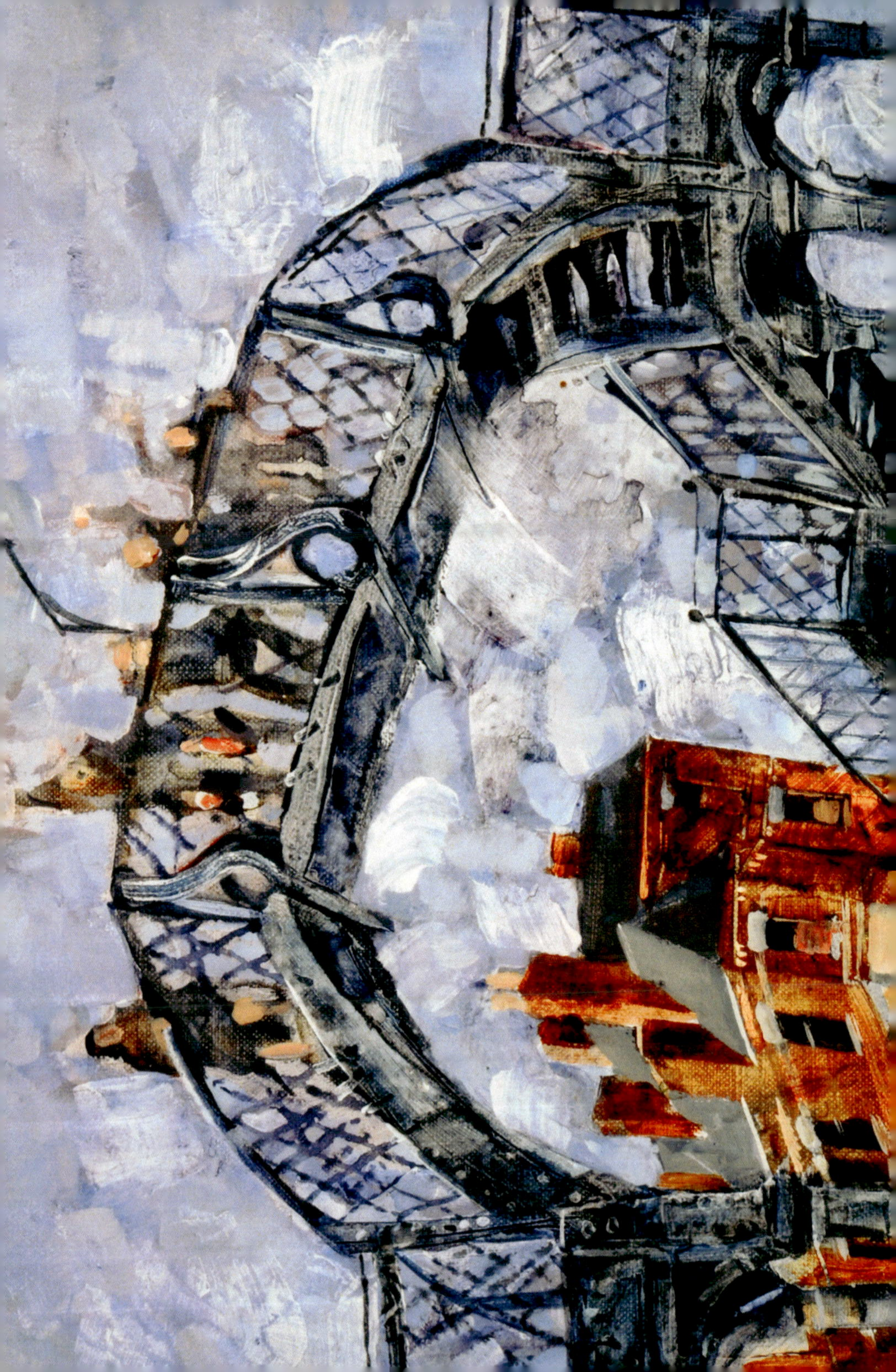

Byron and the Byronic

Bertrand Russell

This Byron Foundation Lecture was delivered at University College, Nottingham on Friday 12 November 1937. Russell specified no title for his Lecture, but suggested 'as subject the development of Byronic romanticism in politics and in ways of feeling – eg Lawrence'. In the event, 'Byron and the Byronic' was the title announced by Nottingham University. How did Russell's warnings sound to his audience during those troubled years?

◀ Paul Waplington is arguably Nottingham's finest living artist, now resident in Portugal. Prints of his work are available to buy at www.paulwaplingtonart.com

The nineteenth century, in comparison with the present age, appears rational, progressive, and satisfied; yet the opposite qualities of our time were possessed by many of the most remarkable men during the epoch of liberal optimism. When we consider men, not as artists or discoverers, not as sympathetic or antipathetic to our own tastes, but as forces, as causes of change in the social structure, in judgements of value, or in intellectual outlook, we find that the course of events in recent times has necessitated much readjustment in our estimates, making some men less important than they had seemed, and others more so. Among those whose importance is greater than it seemed, I shall maintain that Byron deserves a high place. On the Continent, such a view would not appear surprising, but in the English-speaking world it may be thought strange. It was on the Continent that Byron was influential, and it is not in England that his spiritual progeny is to be sought. To most of us, his verse seems often poor and his sentiment often tawdry, but abroad his way of feeling and his outlook on life were transmitted and developed and transmuted until they became so widespread as to be factors in great events.

The aristocratic rebel, of whom Byron was in his day the exemplar, is a very different type from the leader of a peasant or proletarian revolt. Those who are hungry have no need of an elaborate philosophy to stimulate or excuse discontent, and anything of the kind appears to them merely an amusement of the idle rich. They want what others have, not some intangible and metaphysical good. Though they may preach Christian love, as the medieval communist rebels did, their real reasons for doing so are very simple: that the lack of it in the rich and powerful causes the sufferings of the poor, and that the presence of it among comrades in revolt is thought essential to success. But experience of the struggle leads to a despair of the powers of love, leaving naked hate as the driving force. A rebel of this type, if, like Marx, he invents a philosophy, invents one solely designed to demonstrate the ultimate victory of his party, not one concerned with values. His values remain primitive: the good is enough to eat, and the rest is talk. No hungry man is likely to think otherwise.

The aristocratic rebel, since he has enough to eat, must have other causes of discontent. I do not include among rebels the mere leaders of factions temporarily out of power; I include only men whose philosophy requires some greater change then their own personal success. It may be that love of power is the underground source of their discontent, but in their conscious thought there is criticism of the government of the world, which, when it goes deep enough, takes the form of Titanic cosmic self-assertion, or, in those who retain some superstition, of Satanism. Both are to be found in Byron. Both, largely through men whom he influenced, became common in large sections of society which could hardly be deemed aristocratic. The aristocratic philosophy of rebellion, growing, developing, and changing as it approached maturity, has inspired a long series of revolutionary movements, from the Carbonari after the fall of Napoleon to Hitler's *coup* in 1933; and at each stage it has inspired a corresponding manner of thought and feeling among intellectuals and artists.

It is obvious that an aristocrat does not become a rebel unless his temperament and circumstances are in some way peculiar. Byron's circumstances were very peculiar. His earliest recollections were of his parents' quarrels; his mother was a woman whom he feared for her cruelty and despised for her vulgarity; his nurse combined wickedness with the strictest Calvinist theology; his lameness filled him with shame, and prevented him from being one of the herd at school. At ten years old, after living in poverty, he suddenly found himself a Lord and the owner of Newstead. His great-uncle the "wicked Lord", from whom he inherited, had killed a man in a duel thirty-three years before, and been ostracized by his neighbours ever since. The Byrons had been a lawless family, and the Gordons, his mother's ancestors, even more so. After the squalor of a back street in Aberdeen, the boy naturally rejoiced in his title and his Abbey, and was willing to take on the character of his ancestors in gratitude for their lands. And if, in recent years, their bellicosity had led them into trouble, he learnt that in former centuries it had brought them renown. One of his earliest poems, "On Leaving Newstead Abbey", relates his emotions at this time:

> Through thy battlements, Newstead, the hollow winds whistle;
> Thou, the hall of my fathers, art gone to decay;
> In thy once smiling garden the hemlock and thistle
> Have choked up the rose which late bloomed in the way.
> Of the mail-covered Barons, who proudly to battle
> Led their vassals from Europe to Palestine's plain,
> The escutcheon and shield, which with every blast rattle,
> Are the only sad vestiges now that remain.

And so on, through Cressy and Marston Moor, until he comes to the moral:

> Shades of heroes, farewell; your descendent, departing
> From the scene of his ancestors, bids you adieu!
> Abroad or at home, your remembrance imparting
> New courage, he'll think upon glory and you.
> Though a tear dim his eye at this sad separation,
> 'Tis nature, not fear, that excites his regret;
> Far distant he goes, with the same emulation,
> The fame of his fathers he ne'er can forget.
> That fame and that memory still will he cherish:
> He vows that he ne'er will disgrace your renown:
> Like you will he live, or like you will he perish:
> When decay'd, may he mingle his dust with your own.

This is not the mood of a rebel, but it suggests "Childe" Harold, the modern peer who imitates medieval Barons. As an undergraduate, when for the first time Byron had an income of his own, he wrote that he felt as independent as "a German Prince who coins his own cash, or a Cherokee Chief who coins no cash at all, but enjoys what is more precious, Liberty. I speak in raptures of that Goddess because my amiable Mama was so despotic". He wrote, in later life, much noble verse in praise of freedom, but it must be understood that the freedom he praised was that of a German Prince or a Cherokee Chief, not the inferior sort that might conceivably be enjoyed by ordinary mortals.

In spite of his lineage and his title, his aristocratic relations fought shy of him, and he was made to feel himself not of their society. His mother was intensely disliked, and he was looked on with suspicion. He knew that she was vulgar, and darkly feared a similar defect in himself. Hence arose that peculiar blend of snobbery and rebellion that characterized him. If he could not be a gentleman in the modern style, he would be a bold baron in the style of his crusading ancestors, or perhaps in the more ferocious but even more romantic style of the Ghibelline chiefs, cursed of God and man as they trampled their way to splendid downfall. Medieval romances and histories were his etiquette books. He sinned like the Hohenstaufen, and like the crusaders he died fighting the Moslem.

His shyness and sense of friendlessness made him look for comfort in love affairs, but as he was unconsciously seeking a mother rather than a mistress, all disappointed him except Augusta. Calvinism, which he never shook off – to Shelley, in 1816, he described himself as "Methodist, Calvinist, Augustinian" – made him feel that his manner of life was wicked; but wickedness, he told himself, was a hereditary curse in his blood, an evil fate to which he was predestined by the Almighty. If that were indeed the case, since he *must* be remarkable, he would be remarkable as a sinner, and would dare transgressions beyond the courage of the fashionable libertines whom he wished to despise. He loved Augusta genuinely because she was of his blood – of the Ishmaelite race of the Byrons – and also, more simply, because she had an elder sister's kindly care for his daily welfare. But this was not all that she had to offer him. Through her simplicity and her obliging good nature, she became the means of providing him with the most delicious self-congratulatory remorse. He could feel himself the equal of the greatest sinners – the peer of Manfred, of Cain, almost of Satan himself. The Calvinist, the aristocrat, and the rebel were all equally satisfied; and so was the romantic lover, whose heart was broken by the loss of the only earthly being still capable of rousing in it the gentler emotions of pity and love.

> She was like me in lineaments – her eyes,
> Her hair, her features, all to the very tone
> Even of her voice, they said were like to mine;
> But softened all, and tempered into beauty:
> She had the same lone thoughts, and wanderings,
> The quest of hidden knowledge, and a mind
> To comprehend the universe: nor these
> Alone, but with them gentler powers than mine,
> Pity, and smiles, and tears – which I had not;
> And tenderness – but that I had for her;
> Humility – and that I never had.

> Her faults were mine – her virtues were her own –
> I loved her, and destroyed her!

But if not humility, he still has pride to comfort him. When the fiend begins: "Thy many crimes have made thee", he interrupts:

> What are they to such as thee?
> Must crimes be punished but by other crimes,
> And greater criminals? – Back to thy hell!
> Thou hast no power upon me, *that* I feel;
> Thou never shalt possess me, *that* I know;
> What I have done is done: I bear within
> A torture which could nothing gain from thine ...
> *Thou* didst not tempt me, and thou could'st not tempt me;
> I have not been thy dupe, nor am thy prey –
> But was my own destroyer, and will be
> My own hereafter – Back, ye baffled fiends!
> The hand of death is on me – but not yours!

Byron, though he felt himself the equal of Satan, never quite ventured to put himself in the place of God. This next step in the growth of pride was taken by Nietzsche, who says: "If there were Gods, how could I endure it to be no God! *Therefore* there are no Gods." Observe the premiss of this reasoning: "Whatever humbles my pride is to be judged false." Nietzsche, like Byron, and even to a greater degree, had a pious upbringing, but having a better intellect, he found a better escape than Satanism. He remained, however, very sympathetic to Byron: "The tragedy is that we cannot believe the dogmas of religion and metaphysics if we have the strict methods of truth in heart and head, but on the other hand we have become through the development of humanity so tenderly sensitively suffering that we need the highest kind of means of salvation and consolation: whence arises the danger that man may bleed to death through the truth that he recognizes." Byron expresses this in immortal lines:

> Sorrow is knowledge: they who know the most
> Must mourn the deepest o'er the fatal truth,
> The Tree of Knowledge is not that of Life.

Sometimes, though rarely, Byron approaches more nearly to Nietzsche's point of view. For example, in Cain, where Lucifer says:

> He as a conqueror will call the conquered
> *Evil*: but what will be the *good* He gives!
> Were I the victor, *His* works would be deemed
> The only evil ones.

But in general Byron's ethical theory, as opposed to his practice, remains strictly conventional.

The great man, to Nietzsche, is godlike; to Byron, usually, a Titan at war with himself. Sometimes, however, he portrays a sage not unlike Zarathustra:

> He who ascends to mountain tops, shall find
> The loftiest peaks most wrapped in cloud and snow;
> He who surpasses or subdues mankind,
> Must look down on the hate of those below.
> Though high *above* the sun of glory glow,
> And far *beneath* the earth and ocean spread,
> *Round* him are icy rocks, and loudly blow
> Contending tempests on his naked head,
> And thus reward the toils which to those summits led.

The Corsair, in his dealings with his followers,

> Still sways their souls with that commanding art
> That dazzles, leads, yet chills the vulgar heart.

And this same hero "hated man too much to feel remorse". A footnote assures us that the Corsair is true to human nature, since similar traits were exhibited by Genseric, King of the Vandals, by Ezzelino the Ghibelline tyrant[1] and by a certain Louisiana pirate.

Byron was not obliged to confine himself to the Levant and the Middle Ages in his search for heroes, since it was not difficult to invest Napoleon with a romantic mantel. The influence of Napoleon on the imagination of nineteenth-century Europe was very profound; he inspired Clausewitz, Stendhal, Heine, the thought of Fichte and the acts of Italian patriots. His ghost stalks through the age, the only force which is strong enough to stand up against industrialism and commerce, pouring scorn on pacifism and shopkeeping. Tolstoy's *War and Peace* is an attempt to exorcise the ghost, but a vain one, for the spectre has never been more powerful than at the present day. Just after Waterloo, Byron summed him up:

> Quiet to quick bosoms is a hell,
> And *there* had been thy bane; there is a fire
> And motion of the soul, which will not dwell
> In its own narrow being, but aspire
> Beyond the fitting medium of desire;
> And, but once kindled, quenchless evermore,
> Preys upon high adventure, nor can tire
> Of aught but rest; a fever at the core,
> Fatal to him who bears, to all who ever bore.

During the Hundred Days, he proclaimed his wish for Napoleon's victory, and when he heard of Waterloo he said "I'm damned sorry for it." Only once, for a moment, did he turn against his hero: in 1814, when (so he thought) suicide would have been more seemly than abdication. At this moment, he sought consolation in the virtue of Washington, but the return from Elba made this effort no longer necessary. In France, when Byron died, "It was remarked in many newspapers that the two greatest men of the century, Napoleon and Byron, had disappeared almost at the same time".[2] Carlyle, who, at the time, considered Byron "the noblest spirit in Europe", and felt as if he had "lost a brother", came afterwards to prefer Goethe, but still coupled Byron with Napoleon:

> For your nobler minds, the publishing of some such Work of Art, in one or the other dialect, becomes almost a necessity. For what is it properly but an altercation with the Devil, before you begin honestly Fighting him? Your Byron publishes his *Sorrows of Lord George*, in verse and in prose, and copiously otherwise: your Bonaparte presents his *Sorrows of Napoleon* Opera, in an all-too stupendous style; with music of cannon-volleys, and murder-shrieks of a world; his stage-lights are the fires of Conflagration; his rhyme and recitative are the tramp of embattled Hosts and the sound of falling Cities.[3]

It is true that, three chapters further on, Carlyle gives the emphatic command: "Close thy *Byron*; open thy *Goethe*." But Byron was in his blood, whereas Goethe remained an aspiration.

To Carlyle, Goethe and Byron were antitheses; to Alfred de Musset, they were accomplices in the wicked work of instilling the poison of melancholy into the cheerful Gallic soul. Most young Frenchmen of that age knew Goethe, it seems, only through the *Sorrows of Werther*, and not at all as the Olympian. Musset blamed Byron for not being consoled by the Adriatic and Countess Guiccioli – wrongly, for after he knew her he wrote no more *Manfreds*. But *Don Juan* was as little read in France as Goethe's more cheerful poetry. What Musset says about the pair is interesting:

> *Or, vers ce temps-là, deux poètes, les deux plus beaux génies du siècle après Napoléon, venaient de consacrer leur vie à rassembler tous les éléments d'angoisse et de douleur épars dans l'univers. Goethe, le patriarche d'une littérature nouvelle, après avoir peint dans Werther la passion qui mène au suicide, avait tracé dans son Faust la plus sombre figure humaine qui eût jamais représenté le mal et le malheur. Ses écrits commencèrent alors à passer d'Allemagne en France. Du fond de son cabinet d'étude, entouré de tableaux et de statues, riche, heureux et tranquille, il regardait venir à nous son oeuvre de ténèbres avec un sourire paternel. Byron lui répondit par un cri de douleur qui fit tressaillir la Grèce, et suspendit Manfred sur les abîmes, comme si le néant eût été le mot de l'énigme hideuse dont il s'enveloppait.*
>
> *Pardonnez-moi, ô grands poètes, qui êtes maintenant un peu de cendre et qui reposez sous la terre! pardonnez-moi! vous êtes des demi-dieux, et je ne suis qu'un enfant qui souffre. Mais, en écrivant tout ceci, je ne puis m'empêcher de vous maudire.* (Translation at end of article)

And he proceeds to tell them that they ought to have made poetry out of their joys as well as their sorrows. But most French poets, ever since, have found Byronic unhappiness the best material for their verses.

It will be observed that, to Musset, it was only after Napoleon that Byron and Goethe were the greatest geniuses of the century. Born in 1810, Musset was one of the generation whom he describes as *conçus entre deux batailles* in a lyrical account of the glories and disasters of the Empire. In Germany, feeling about Napoleon was more divided. There were those who, like Heine, saw him as the mighty missionary of liberalism, the destroyer of serfdom, the enemy of legitimacy, the man who made hereditary princelings tremble; there were others who saw him as Antichrist, the would-be destroyer of the noble German nation, the immoralist who had proved once for all that Teutonic virtue can only be preserved by unquenchable hatred of France. Bismarck effected a synthesis: Napoleon remained Antichrist, but an Antichrist to be imitated, not merely to be abhorred. Nietzsche, who accepted the compromise, remarked with ghoulish joy that the classical age of war is coming, and that we owe this boon, not to the French Revolution, but to Napoleon. And in this way nationalism, Satanism, and hero-worship, the legacy of Byron, became part of the complex soul of Germany.

Mary Shelley's *Frankenstein*, written under the inspiration of conversations with Byron in the romantic scenery of the Alps, contains what might almost be regarded as an allegorical prophetic history of the development of romanticism. Frankenstein's monster is not, as he has become in proverbial parlance, a mere monster: he is, at first, a gentle being, longing for human affection, but he is driven to hatred and violence by the horror which his ugliness inspires in those whose love he attempts to gain. Unseen, he observes a virtuous family of poor cottagers, and surreptitiously assists their labours. At length he decides to make himself known to them:

> The more I saw of them, the greater became my desire to claim their protection and kindness; my heart yearned to be known and loved by these amiable creatures: to see their sweet looks directed towards me with affection, was the utmost limit of my ambition. I dared not think that they would turn from me with disdain and horror.

But they did. So he first demanded of his creator the creation of a female like himself, and, when that was refused, devoted himself to murdering, one by one, all whom Frankenstein loved. But even then, when all his murders are accomplished, and while he is gazing upon the dead body of Frankenstein, the monster's *sentiments* remain noble:

> That also is my victim! in his murder my crimes are consummated: the miserable series of my being is wound to its close! Oh, Frankenstein! generous and self-devoted being! What does it avail that I now ask thee to pardon me? I, who irretrievably destroyed thee by destroying all that thou lovedst. Alas! he is cold, he cannot answer me ... He (he continued, pointing to the corpse) he suffered not in the consummation of the death – oh! not the ten-thousandth portion of the anguish that was mine during the lingering detail of its execution. A frightful selfishness hurried me on, while my heart was poisoned with remorse. Think you that the groans of Clerval were music to my ears? My heart (he said of himself) was fashioned to be susceptible of love and sympathy; and, when wrenched by misery, and vice and hatred, it did not endure the violence of the change, without torture such as you cannot even imagine ... When I run over the frightful catalogue of my sins, I cannot believe that I am the same creature whose thoughts were once filled with sublime and transcendent visions of the beauty and the majesty of goodness. But it is even so; the fallen angel becomes a malignant devil. Yet even that enemy of God and man had friends and associates in his desolation; I am alone.

Robbed of its romantic form, there is nothing unreal in this psychology, and it is unnecessary to search out pirates or Vandal kings in order to find parallels. To an English visitor, the ex-Kaiser, at Doorn, lamented that the English no longer loved him. Dr. Burt, in his book on the juvenile delinquent, mentions a boy of seven who drowned another boy in the Regent's Canal. His reason was that neither his family nor his contemporaries showed him affection. Dr. Burt was kind to him, and he became a respectable citizen; but no Dr. Burt undertook the reformation of Frankenstein's monster.

It is not the psychology of the romantics that is at fault: it is their standard of values. They admire strong passions, of no matter what kind, and whatever may be their social consequences. Romantic love, especially when unfortunate, is strong enough to win their approval, but most of the strongest passions are destructive – hate and resentment and jealousy, remorse and despair, outraged pride and the fury of the unjustly oppressed, martial ardour and contempt for slaves and cowards. Hence the type of man encouraged by romanticism, especially of the Byronic variety, is violent and anti-social, an anarchic rebel or a conquering tyrant.

This outlook makes an appeal for which the reasons lie very deep in human nature and human circumstances. By self-interest Man has become gregarious, but in instinct he has remained to a great extent solitary; hence the need of religion and morality to reinforce self-interest. But the habit of forgoing present satisfactions for the sake of future advantages is irksome, and when passions are roused the prudent restraints of social behaviour become difficult to endure. Those who, at such times, throw them off, acquire a new energy and sense of power from the cessation of inner conflict, and, though they may come to disaster in the end, enjoy meanwhile a sense of godlike exaltation which, though known to the great mystics, can never be experienced by a merely pedestrian virtue. The solitary part of their nature reasserts itself, but if the intellect survives, the reassertion must clothe itself in myth. The mystic becomes one with God, and in the contemplation of the Infinite feels himself absolved from duty to his neighbour. The anarchic rebel does even better: he feels himself not one with God, but God. Truth and duty, which represent our subjection to matter and to our neighbours, exist no longer for the man who has become God; for others, truth is what *he* posits, duty what *he* commands. If we could all live solitary and without labour, we could all enjoy this ecstasy of independence; since we cannot, its delights are only available to madmen and dictators.

The romantic movement is, in essence, a revolt of our solitary instincts against the difficult precepts of social co-operation. Such social relations as we share with gorillas – sexual love and family affection – are spared by the earlier forms of romanticism, because their hold upon our instincts is very strong; but other restrictions imposed by society are loosened one by one. First comes the revolt against etiquette and the formal manners of Courts, the "return to nature" and the belief in the simple virtues of the peasant. With this (not from observation of peasants) goes the belief that sexual relations should be based on love and an attack upon the customs of making marriage an economic contract. At the same time there is admiration for pastoral scenery as opposed to that of Fleet Street, which Dr. Johnson preferred, and there is a revolt against artificial forms in art and literature. All this had happened before Byron's time, and since it attacked nothing essential to the social structure it was not open to serious criticism.

But, under the stimulus of the French Revolution and the Napoleonic wars, revolt went deeper. The change is typified by the change in scenery. Byron no longer writes of mossy glades and sylvan rivulets; he writes of deserts and Alps, of thunderstorms and shipwrecks:

> O night
> And storm and darkness, ye are wondrous strong....
> Far along,
> From peak to peak, the rattling crags among,
> Leaps the live thunder!

All this, he says, is like "the light of a dark eye in woman"; love, for him, is not gentle, but violent like a thunderstorm. What Byron says of Rousseau is applicable to himself. Rousseau was, he says,

> He who threw
> Enchantment over passion, and from woe
> Wrung overwhelming eloquence ... yet he knew
> How to make madness beautiful, and cast
> O'er erring deeds and thoughts, a heavenly hue.

But there is a profound difference between the two men. Rousseau is pathetic, Byron is fierce; Rousseau's timidity is obvious, Byron's is concealed; Rousseau admires virtue provided it is simple, while Byron admires sin provided it is elemental. The difference, thought it is only that between two stages in the revolt of unsocial instincts, is important, and shows the direction in which the movement is developing.

Revolt of solitary instincts against social bonds is the key to the philosophy, the politics, and the sentiments, not only of what is commonly called the romantic movement, but of its progeny down to the present day. Philosophy, under the influence of German idealism, became solipsistic, and self-development was proclaimed as the fundamental principles of ethics.[4] As regards sentiment, there has to be a distasteful compromise between the search for isolation and the necessities of passion and economics. D. H. Lawrence's story, "The Man Who Loved Islands", has a hero who disdained such compromise to a gradually increasing extent, and at last died of hunger and cold, but in the enjoyment of complete isolation; but this degree of consistency has not been achieved by the writers who praise solitude. The comforts of civilized life are not obtainable by a hermit, and a man who wishes to write books or produce works of art must submit to the ministrations of others if he is to survive while he does his work. In order to continue to *feel* solitary, he must be able to prevent those who serve him from impinging upon his ego, which is best accomplished if they are slaves. Passionate love, however, is a more difficult matter. So long as passionate lovers are regarded as in revolt against social trammels, they are admired; but in real life the love-relation itself quickly becomes a social trammel, and the partner in love comes to be hated, all the more vehemently if the love is strong enough to make the bond difficult to break. Hence love comes to be conceived as a battle, in which each is attempting to destroy the other by breaking through the protecting walls of his or her ego. This point of view has become familiar through the writings of Strindberg, and, still more, of D. H. Lawrence.

Not only passionate love, but every friendly relation to others, is only possible, to this way of feeling, in so far as the others can be regarded as a projection of one's own Self. This is feasible if the others are blood-relations, and the more nearly they are related the more easily it is possible. Hence an emphasis on race, leading, as in the case of the Ptolemys, to endogamy. How this affected Byron, we know; Wagner suggests a similar sentiment in the love of Siegmund and Sieglinde. Nietzsche, though not scandalously, preferred his sister to all other women: "How strongly I feel," he writes to her, "in all that you say and do, that we belong to the same stock. You understand more of me than others do, because we come of the same parentage. This fits in very well with my 'philosophy'."

The principle of nationality, of which Byron was a protagonist, is an extension of the same "philosophy". A nation is assumed to be a race, descended from common ancestors, and sharing some kind of "blood-consciousness". Mazzini, who constantly found fault with the English for their failure to appreciate Byron, conceived nations as possessed of a mystical individuality, and attributed to them the kind of anarchic greatness that other romantics sought in heroic men. Liberty, for nations, came to be regarded, not only by Mazzini, but by comparatively sober statesmen, as something absolute, which, in practice, made international co-operation impossible.

Belief in blood and race is naturally associated with anti-Semitism. At the same time, the romantic outlook, partly because it is aristocratic, and partly because it prefers passion to calculation, has a vehement contempt for commerce and finance. It is thus led to proclaim an opposition to capitalism which is quite different from that of the socialist who represents the interest of the proletariat, since it is an opposition based on dislike of economic preoccupations, and strengthened by the suggestion that the capitalist world is governed by Jews. This point of view is expressed by Byron on the rare occasions when he condescends to notice anything so vulgar as economic power:

> Who hold the balance of the world? Who reign
> O'er congress, whether royalist or liberal? ...
> Who rouse the shirtless patriots of Spain?
> (That make old Europe's journals squeak and gibber all.)
> Who keep the world, both Old and New, in pain
> Or Pleasure? Who make politics run glibber all?
> The shade of Buonaparte's noble daring?
> Jew Rothschild, and his fellow Christian Baring.

The verse is perhaps not very musical, but the sentiment is quite of our time.

To sum up, the romantic movement, in which Byron was the most romantic figure, aimed at liberating human personality from the fetters of social convention and social morality. In part, these fetters were a mere useless hindrance to desirable forms of activity, for every ancient community has developed rules of behaviour for which there is nothing to be said except that they are traditional. But egoistic passions, when once let loose, are not easily brought again into subjection to the needs of society. Christianity had succeeded, to some extent, in taming the Ego, but economic, political, and intellectual causes stimulated revolt against the churches, and the romantic movement brought the revolt into the sphere of morals. By encouraging a new lawless Ego it made social co-operation impossible, and left its disciples faced with the alternative of anarchy or despotism. Egoism, at first, as in Frankenstein's monster, made men expect from others a parental tenderness; but when they discovered, with indignation, that others had their own Ego, the disappointed desire for tenderness turned to hatred and violence. Man is not a solitary animal, and, so long as social life survives, self-realization cannot be the supreme principle of ethics.

* * *

Musset translation:

Now, about this time, two poets, the two most beautiful geniuses of the century after Napoleon, had just consecrated their lives to gather all the elements of anguish and pain scattered in the universe. Goethe, the patriarch of a new literature, after having painted in Werther the passion which leads to suicide, had drawn in his Faust the darkest human figure who had ever represented evil and misfortune. His writings then began to move from Germany to France. From the depths of his study-room, surrounded by pictures and statues, rich, happy and tranquil, he watched his work of darkness come to us with a paternal smile. Byron replied with a cry of sorrow that made Greece tremble, and suspended Manfred on the abyss, as if nothing had been the word of the hideous enigma of his wrapping. Forgive me, O great poets, who are now a little ashes and who rest under the earth! excuse me! you are demi-gods, and I am only a child who suffers. But, in writing all this, I can not help but curse you.

Notes:

1. Whom Dante finds in hell, among the "tyrants who took to blood and plunder". *Inferno*, Canto XII.
2. Maurois, *Life of Byron*.
3. *Sartor Resartus*, Book II, Chap. VI.
4. Papini, in his youth a disciple of William James, and afterwards one of the philosophic champions of Fascism, wrote, in his early period, an essay called "L'Imitazione d'Iddio", in which he urges that we should henceforth take, not Christ, but God the Father, as our model.

* * *

Irrationalism

'Although Russell had a longstanding interest in the historical roots of the irrationalism he saw disfiguring the inter-war world, a more proximate stimulus for this essay had come in the form of an invitation to speak at the University of Nottingham, which Russell received from the psychologist (and fellow Cambridge Apostle) W.J.H. Sprott. In confirming this engagement, Russell supplied Sprott with no definite title for his talk but suggested 'as subject the development of Byronic romanticism in politics and in ways of feeling – eg Lawrence'. The lecture was delivered ... [on 12 November 1937], when Russell informed Sprott that he would travel to Nottingham by train from his new home near Oxford ...

... Russell had developed a keen interest in establishing the connection between the romantic legacy and the most disturbing ideological currents in circulation in the 1930s. Some time after rereading Mary Shelley's Frankenstein *for the essay on Byron, he described that classic work to Lady Ottoline Morrell as 'a prophetic history of the whole romantic movement, which has culminated in Hitler' (8 February 1938)... Especially deplorable, according to Russell, was the Byronic fervour for 'strong passions, of no matter what kind, and whatever may be their social consequences ...'

Source: Collected Papers of Bertrand Russell, Volume 21, *edited by Andrew G Bone and Michael D Stevenson, pages 254-255*

Harting 6.

Telegraph House
Harting, Petersfield.

7.11.37

Dear Sprott

To my surprise, I find there are through expresses from Oxford to Nottingham almost every few minutes. I propose to take one which arrives at 4.45. I am told I don't need to dress for the lecture.

Yours sincerely
Bertrand Russell.

▲ 'Dear Sprott' letter. Source: Russell Archives, McMaster University, Canada

In December 1961, the British fascist, Oswald Mosley, sent Bertrand Russell two of his books. Mosley wrote of 'the two root differences between us' in international politics, and subsequently invited Russell to lunch. On 22 January 1962, Russell declined the invitation in these terms.

Dear Sir Oswald,

Thank you for your letter and for your enclosures. I have given some thought to our recent correspondence. It is always difficult to decide on how to respond to people whose ethos is so alien and, in fact, repellent to one's own. It is not that I take exception to the general points made by you but that every ounce of my energy has been devoted to an active opposition to cruel bigotry, compulsive violence, and the sadistic persecution which has characterised the philosophy and practice of fascism.

I feel obliged to say that the emotional universes we inhabit are so distinct, and in deepest ways opposed, that nothing fruitful or sincere could ever emerge from association between us.

I should like you to understand the intensity of this conviction on my part. It is not out of any attempt to be rude that I say this but because of all that I value in human experience and human achievement.

Yours sincerely,

Bertrand Russell

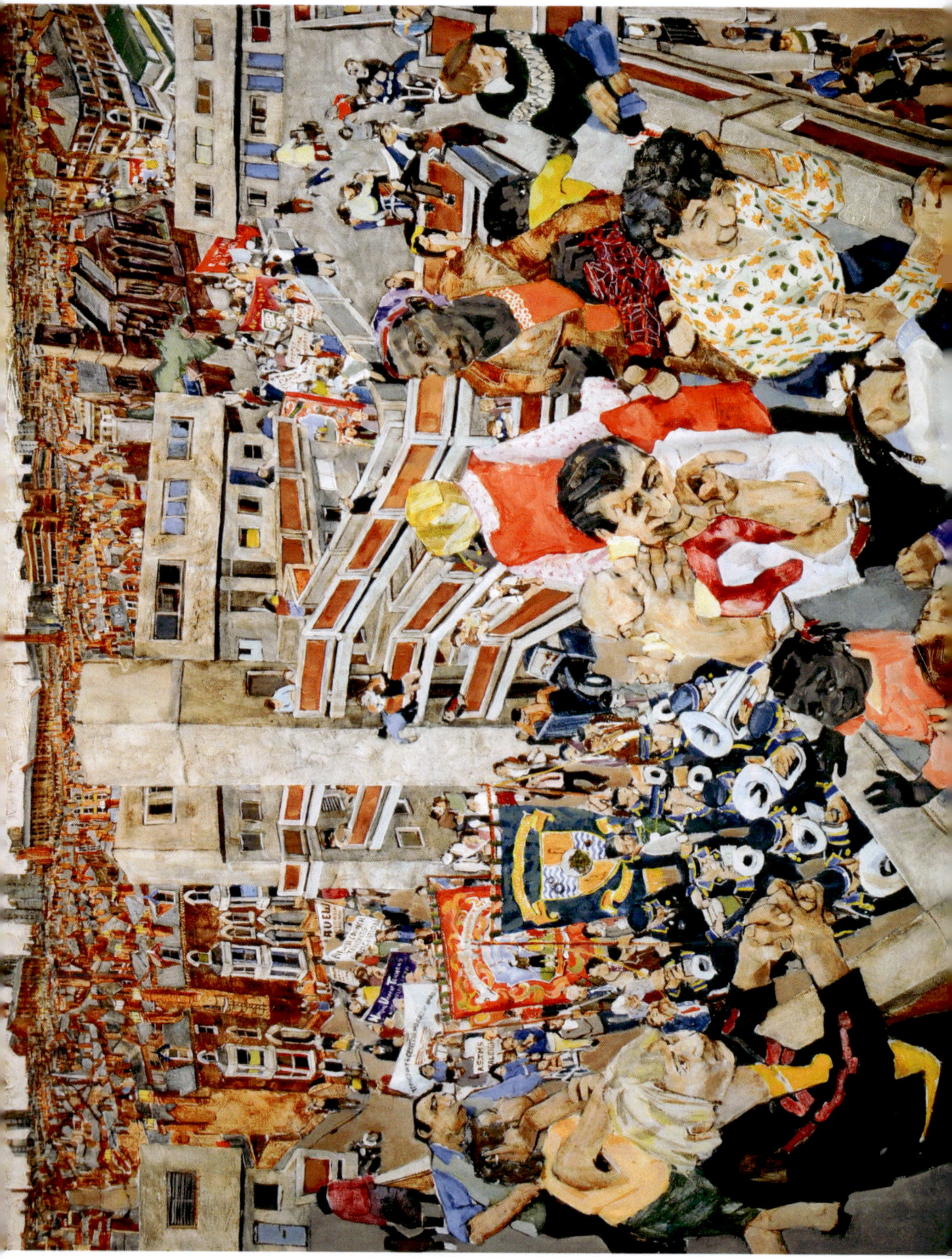

Inside the Goldmine

Daniel Jakopovich

Daniel Jakopovich is from Croatia. He is a writer, poet and campaigner for peace, human rights and animal liberation. This article is taken from his new book, Revolutionary Peacemaking: Writings for a Culture of Peace and Nonviolence, *published by Democratic Thought (democraticthought.org). Full notes and references can be found in this book.*

◄ Paul Waplington, *May Day,* Hyson Green, Nottingham

Obstacles to the Construction of Enlightened Democratic Self-Government in Former Yugoslavia[1]

"The nearest approach to purest anarchy would be a democracy based on nonviolence"
Mohandas Karamchand Gandhi

"Men [sic] may be trusted to govern themselves without a master"
Thomas Jefferson

In 1950 the Federal Assembly of Yugoslavia formally inaugurated workers' self-management by passing the *Basic Law on the Management of State Economic Enterprises and Higher Economic Associations by Workers' Collectives*. The Yugoslav socialist "experiment", indubitably a remarkable example of historical creativity, is still a goldmine of insights and experiences. As it is useful to learn about the positive aspects of this experience, it is also important to learn from its mistakes and limitations. This article offers some fairly cursory notes which aim to introduce a vast subject.

The most visionary minds of the Yugoslav revolution advanced the concept of workers' self-management and, subsequently, of workers' and citizens' integral self-government (socialist democracy) on the basis of the principles of equal self-determination and of human self-actualisation. These entail the right of all citizens to be the self-governing, consciously and rationally cooperative protagonists of the historical process, the conscious and cooperative creators of a freer, more advanced human community, rather than being merely reduced to the position of objects of capitalist rule[2]. In other words, democratic self-government is the democratically cooperative, socially coordinated expression of the principles of human dignity and equal self-determination.

Stipe Šuvar, a leading Marxist sociologist who was the Vice President of Yugoslavia and the (broadly democratic socialist and staunchly anti-nationalist) Chair of the League of Communists of Yugoslavia (which was previously called the Communist Party), used to, only partially in jest, describe the Yugoslav experience, in accordance with its underdeveloped material and social reality, as a form of "shepherds' self-government". Yugoslavia's socialist development was seriously hindered by the rather marginal position of the working class in its economic and social structure: around 75% of the Yugoslav population were peasants prior to the Second World War. One of the Yugoslav Communist leaders and perhaps the single most important architect of the Yugoslav system of popular "self-government", Edvard Kardelj, noted that Yugoslav pre-WWII electricity production was (supposedly) 59 times below the European average. The immense misery, brutality and destruction brought about by WWII also in many ways severely degraded the material and subjective components on which the prospect for the foundation of peaceful and humane democratic socialism is based. Among the basic constraints in relation to this were also the requirements of post-war reconstruction[3], industrialisation and urbanisation, which reinforced the centralist character of social organisation and deflected human and other resources from higher-level activities and projects on which the construction of a higher type of civilisation depends.

In terms of the weakness of the "revolutionary subjective forces", the Communist Party of Yugoslavia was subjected to close oversight by the Soviet Union and was forced to operate underground under a highly centralised command structure for more than twenty years, from 1920 (when it was banned, having just made a significant electoral breakthrough in the general parliamentary elections in the Kingdom of Yugoslavia) to 1945. This reinforced anti-democratic, hyper-centralist patterns, precluding the free and open development of the Yugoslav socialist and labour movement, let alone of more radical peacemaking social forces. The broad population lacked sufficient experience in the struggle for self-emancipation. It was often still wedded to rural cultural, ideological and lifestyle patterns and it lacked the necessary self-organisation and self-confidence, class consciousness, the requisite educational level and democratic and revolutionary peacemaking political culture. The Stalinist practices of the Communist Party, particularly before its split with Stalin and the Eastern Bloc in 1948, certainly did not help in this regard.

Some have identified the origins of socialist innovation which characterised post-WWII Yugoslav development in the anti-fascist "committees of national liberation" that operated during the war. These were formed in 1941 as organs of dual power constituted through direct popular elections as an expression of autonomous anti-fascist initiative in Yugoslavia. They existed legally in liberated territories and operated underground in those territories that were still occupied. Leading communists such as Moša Pijade and Kardelj later characterised these anti-fascist committees as the first nascent forms epitomising the Yugoslav independent, non-Stalinist course[4]. Yugoslavia's subsequent alternative path was indeed made possible by the fairly autonomous character of the Yugoslav struggle against Fascism and Nazism. Additionally, the various immense sacrifices, including the fact that many Yugoslav socialists and communists were systematically persecuted, subjected to torture and given long prison sentences in the Kingdom of Yugoslavia, that around a hundred leading Yugoslav communists (as well as one of Josip Broz Tito's wives) had been murdered in Stalin's purges and camps in the Soviet Union between the world wars, and that around a million Yugoslavs appear to have died in the war – including around 300,000 partisan fighters, around 50,000 party members and around 75 per cent of the party's pre-war cadres – must have strengthened the resolve of a critical mass of Yugoslav revolutionaries and of the wider population to forge their own destiny.

The anti-fascist struggle had unleashed powerful (although routinely quite primitive) popular initiative and democratic energy. In reality, however, it was only after the historical split with the Soviet Union and the rest of the Eastern Bloc in 1948 (which was provoked by Stalin's and the Cominform's attempt to depose the Yugoslav leadership or to force it to submit to his diktat) that a resolutely anti-Stalinist alternative road began to be paved. The rather innovative Yugoslav leaders had to legitimise their shift in ideological terms, and they benefited from broad popular support for the principle of international equality in opposition to the Soviet Moloch. The Yugoslav leaders looked back to earlier attempts to institute workers' self-government (such as the Paris Commune, the Russian revolutionary soviets and factory councils, etc.). This initial period of retrospection, introspection and innovation led to the abandonment of the forced collectivisation of agriculture and culminated in the aforementioned initial law (in 1950) which led to the inchoate socialisation of most nationalised industries[5]. The first workers' council had been established only a year before in the Croatian coastal town of Solin near Split.

"Workers' self-management" was one of the central and foundational features of the Yugoslav anti-capitalist project[6]. Its major aim (especially in theory) was to abolish hierarchical economic relations through a debureaucratisation of enterprises by which the old socialist slogan "factories to the workers" would be implemented. The basic institutional framework of the system of "workers' self-management", which was the ideological term given to the newly instituted workers' participation in company and workplace decision-making (that was eventually introduced in all publicly owned Yugoslav enterprises, i.e. the vast majority of enterprises), commenced with the formation and activity of workers' councils and it was, on the basis of various experiences (some of which I shall later briefly discuss), in the 1960s and especially the 1970s developed and expanded into an integral institutional system of "workers' self-management". Alongside workers' councils as the indirect delegate organs of "self-management", this system also encompassed forms of direct participation of all workers in management through workers' assemblies and through occasional referendums, both of which took place in the basic organisations of associated labour[7].

Workers' assemblies, which encompassed all workers, were (normatively speaking) sovereign assemblies that met occasionally in order to discuss and approve basic matters, including proposed yearly plans, investment plans, reports on last year's results, and similar issues related to the general direction of the company. These assemblies also nominated candidates for workers' councils, who were subsequently elected by all workers through secret ballot[8].

Although the limited degree of actual power and influence of the workers in the workers' assemblies and councils precluded the actualisation of real workers' self-management at the workplace and company levels, their very existence (as well as the fact that the concept of workers' self-management was a central part of the dominant social ideology in post-WWII Yugoslavia) helped to keep the behaviour of the managers (as well as of the workers' delegates on the workers' councils, which ranged from those on the level of the basic organisations of associated labour to the big workers' councils of complex large companies with complex organisational structures) partially in check, thus supporting their (partial) democratic accountability. This was especially so in cases where workers were sufficiently conscious and organised to insist on their positions and interests. The significant degree of redistribution of wealth in favour of the working class is also indicative of the significant economic empowerment of workers which the Yugoslav system, including its workers' councils, brought about.

Company management was, however, also accountable to state organs and laws. Furthermore, notwithstanding the democratic authority of the institutions of workers' self-management, the bureaucratic elite largely retained its hierarchically superior coordinative and supervisory role, which was often also ideologically legitimated as a protection of wider social interests. Company directors were initially appointed by government bodies and were subsequently, perhaps especially until the democratising turn which culminated in the new Constitution in 1974, *de facto* "selected" (i.e. nominated and sponsored) by the ruling political elites from the local to the federal levels, depending on the size and significance of the company in question. In 1974, workers' councils gained the right to elect (by a two-thirds majority) company directors and management boards, as well as to draft statutes of their enterprises, enact their company's economic policies, and to define measures for their implementation. Managerial board members were nominated by "special commissions composed of workers' delegates, members of trade unions, and representatives of socio-political communities (municipalities)". Members of the workers' councils were elected biennially through a secret ballot. However, there was initially no formal obligation on their part to follow the work collectives' wishes on particular issues, although they were subject to recall and their meetings were usually open to every member of the working collective who wanted to attend. The formal introduction of the delegate system in the 1970s gave workers' assemblies a *de facto* although not a *de jure* right to "give council members obligatory instructions how to vote". Hundreds of thousands of workers in Yugoslavia experienced being a member of a workers' council at some point, and millions participated in workers' assemblies.

In the more mature phase of the nascent system of "self-management" (which, roughly speaking, commenced during the 1960s, especially with the Constitution of 1963 which sought to advance the integration of Yugoslav society on a self-governing basis by *officially* introducing self-government "as the general principle of government in all social activities and [territorially-based] socio-political communities"), the general membership of a work organisation or their delegates in the workers' council (which met once or twice a month) held decisive formal decision-making power in relation to all the major functions of an enterprise. This formally included veto power and decision-making power over tenure, hiring and dismissal of all employees, including managerial personnel. It was only from 1963-65 that "self-managing" work organisations began to take control of (a part of) extended reproduction, although at least in some cases they hadn't yet mastered simple reproduction either, i.e. they did not have decisive influence over the determination of wage levels.

Yet, as already noted, workers' assemblies and councils did not exist in isolation from other powerful, even dominant, policy protagonists. They tended to be, at best (!), partial co-managers alongside professionals and managers of companies and institutions who were, in the normative division of labour, supposed to execute the decisions of the workers' council, to deal with the day-to-day functioning of the companies as executive officers. However, evidence indicates that company management tended to guide most economic decision-making, while workers tended to be especially engaged with issues relating to welfare, employment and income allocation. Workers' formal participation rights typically failed to translate into effective participation and control due to various disparities in material, social and cultural power between people in different class positions and with different class backgrounds. Workers' frequent lack of "cultural capital" was one major factor limiting the development of their democratic consciousness, of their social aspirations and of their motivation to actively participate in decision-making, which was – regardless of the significant increase in the ability of workers to influence decision-making – conducive to the continuation of oligarchic and cliquish decision-making patterns in which the company directors and management boards remained dominant. This was in collaboration with various anti-democratic centres of social power/bureaucratic and technocratic interest groups in the community and in the wider society. Šuvar observed that "the self-managing organs have authority more formally than in reality, while the professional organs of management have authority more in reality than formally". Šuvar's observation was based on the fundamental insight that formal authority is not the same as real social power.

Various forms of civic participation were advanced as well. Citizens' assemblies gave all adults (especially normatively but often also *de facto*) the right to direct democratic participation in decision-making over major municipal policies, while other directly elected representatives and delegates carried out various regular local council functions.

In the context of social innovation and ongoing democratisation, Yugoslavia continued its reconstruction, managing to achieve a remarkable level of growth and development, a transformation from a poor, rural semi-colony into a (in relative terms) strongly independent and internationally influential, medium-developed industrialised country (although with acute regional and national inequalities and disparities, which were a major source of nationalist tensions). Major progress was made in terms of elevating the living standard of the masses, including in the fields of education, health care, workers' rights and social security. Social welfare, socialised (i.e. public rather than fully democratised) education, health care and housing were on a world-class level. In fact, Yugoslav workers appear to have enjoyed the highest level of workers' rights in the world (although, of course, not the highest material standard of living). It is important to note that Yugoslav economic development illustrates the possibility of achieving a very high level of efficiency and productivity in a post-capitalist system. Yugoslav social gains were to a large extent dependent on increased material prosperity. In the first few post-WWII decades, Yugoslavia swiftly and powerfully developed its productive forces[9] and urbanised its population[10]. For a time in the 1960s, it had the highest level of GDP growth after Japan and Israel. Clearly, this is a very strong argument against claims that industrial democracy/workers' participation is inherently economically "inefficient". Estrin posited that the partial replacement of conflictual with cooperative forms of economic relationships may have been a contributory factor in the rapid increase in labour productivity in Yugoslavia in the 1950s and 1960s[11]. In his renowned book *The Political Economy of Socialism,* Branko Horvat identified several comparative advantages of democratically-controlled social ownership, including the transcendence of antagonistic interests which impede the dealienation/humanisation of work and can lower efficiency. He also identified the compatibility of non-hierarchical, participatory democratic organisation of work with modern, highly-qualified and creative teamwork, in addition to highlighting the greater accountability of management in socialised enterprises[12] and the more balanced and equitable distribution of wealth. These factors increase the scope for the democratisation of the entire society. More recently, Elinor Ostrom received the Nobel Prize (for which Horvat himself was nominated in 1977 by the American Society of Economists) for her work showing that sustainable and communal self-managed cooperatives are a very efficient alternative to private and state ownership.

Notes
1. I dedicate this study to my father Ivan Jakopović, a socialist intellectual and a creative participant in the Yugoslav socialist revolution, who taught me so much. His insights regarding this topic were invaluable.
2. The movement for democratic self-government challenges the capitalist order both in terms of negating the overt class relationships of domination and submission and in terms of challenging the mystifying phenomena of alienation, reification and commodity fetishism, which impede the conscious democratic control over social processes: "The essence of commodity structure has often been pointed out. Its basis is that a relation between people takes on the character of a thing and thus acquires a 'phantom objectivity', an autonomy that seems so strictly rational and all-embracing as to conceal every trace of its fundamental nature: the relation between people" (Lukacs, 1923).
3. According to Yugoslav and international sources, over 36 per cent of industry was destroyed in the war, as well as 50 per cent of railways and over 800,000 buildings.
4. Moša Pijade (1949) wrote that the setting up of these committees of national liberation showed that "the Communist Party of Yugoslavia from the very beginning had a clear understanding that ensuring the final success of the popular struggle required the smashing of the old machinery of state power and its replacement with new organs of people's power. No other communist party in occupied Europe had the strength to do this".
5. Kardelj (1951) wrote: "The process of the withering away of the state, which is one of the key elements of socialist development, is not spontaneous. To leave this process to spontaneous development is to strengthen reactionary factors which are opposing this process. It would primarily strengthen the bureaucratic tendencies to subordinate the entire society to a centralised state apparatus, a bureaucratic caste in the last instance. (...) Experiences from the current period tell us that bureaucratism is the last and most resilient fortress of the remnants of the class system, and therefore also the most dangerous enemy of socialism".
6. It is very important to bear in mind that workers' self-management and democratic self-government were normative concepts which were never fully realised.
7. Only the very small private sector companies (private companies were not allowed by law to employ more than ten people) did not have to abide by these rules concerning workers' self-management.
8. In small enterprises with less than thirty workers all of them were members of the workers' council. In 1956 central workers' councils were supplemented with workers' councils on the plant and lower levels.
9. The share of agriculture in Yugoslavia's GDP declined from 42.6 per cent in 1947 to 18.8 per cent in 1972, while the share of industry increased from 18.0 to 38.1 per cent in the same period.
10. "In three decades the pyramid of the social structure turned on its head: there were almost 80 per cent of peasants, while today almost 80 per cent of those belonging to the new generations are learning non-agricultural professions and trades with the perspective of becoming entirely urbanised" (Šuvar, S. in Raičević, 1975).
11. In this context, it is interesting to note that Yugoslav workers producing electrical appliances were found to have had higher scores than their Japanese counterparts in relation to measurements of their sense of belonging to their enterprises.
12. Capitalist companies can operate on the brink of bankruptcy – and even go bankrupt – before the stock market starts registering this, without management being open and accountable even to its shareholders, let alone to the workers and to the wider society.

Focus on Europe

Farage's Brexit Party campaign in the elections for the European Parliament has prepared the ground and climate for Boris Johnson and indeed any Tory leader to tread so easily down the reactionary path of right wing nationalism. The rise of Yaxley-Lennon and all the associated alt right movements in the UK and across Europe is clearly deeply worrying. Faced with these prospects isn't it just desperately time the Left woke up?

While the Left is engaged in, at times, a quite bitter wrangle over the question of whether to remain or leave the institutions of the EU, the hard right is seeking to gain new ground and the Tory harsh right is seeking to gain a renewed grip on British politics overall.

I have confessed that I am at heart a Remainer. My reason is that despite the ascendancy of neo-liberalism deep within the institutional settlement of the EU, I recognise that if we are to defeat the hegemony of neo-liberal politics the challenge will not succeed if it is attempted in just one country. The socialist movement learned some time ago to its cost that socialism in one country is not a runner.

The institutional architecture of the EU provides the Left with a significant arena in which the international socialist challenge to neo-liberalism could be played out. In a recent article in *The Spokesman*, Stuart Holland, the former Labour MP and adviser to various European politicians, has described the history of the many attempts by the European Left to promote a socialist alternative across Europe. He outlines the various transnational alliances of socialists that have been formed over the years because of their involvement in the institutional framework of the EU.

However, whatever institutional and constitutional arrangements for our relationship with the rest of Europe come out of the current impasse, as socialists we must ensure that our movement remains an internationalist movement. For us the priority is relationships, not institutions.

The relationships we need to forge urgently now are with all those across Europe who are willing to confront the rise of the right. We must not stand by and allow the newly confident right to bring about a new dark age over Europe.

If this sounds like preaching, it most certainly is. So here is the lesson. There is a hierarchy of political issues.

The rise of the right in all its forms from the alt right to the Boris Johnson harsh Tory right is the real and imminent threat. The institutional arrangements for our economic relationship with the other 27 EU states is an important but subsidiary question compared to the seriousness of the prospect of the long term political dominance of the renewed right within our country and across Europe. And it should be an issue for quiet debate and not highly emotional division.

Moral of this story? Let's focus on the real enemy and the real issue. It's the right and its rise.

John McDonnell MP
Shadow Chancellor

from *Labour Briefing* June 2019

* * *

'A system of employee funds, with a combination of self-management and of influence not limited to the specific enterprise, while at the same time maintaining the state as holder of general authority, is the model for a third, hitherto untried, democratic socialist way.'

Rudolf Meidner, 1980

NPT Dossier
Iran
China

These papers highlight two key issues facing both proponents of nuclear disarmament and nuclear armed states themselves. The first, on the question of a nuclear-weapon-free zone in the Middle East, makes clear the ongoing 'double-standards' at play with regard to the question of non-proliferation and nuclear security in the region. It also spells out the pressing need, and ongoing desire, for a non-nuclear zone. The second working paper alights on the question of 'no first use' and the importance of such a commitment for nuclear security.

1. Establishment of a nuclear-weapon-free zone in the Middle East

Working paper submitted by the Islamic Republic of Iran

The NPT struggles on. The 2019 Peparatory Committee (PrepCom) for the 2020 Nuclear Non-Proliferation Treaty (NPT) Review Conference took place in New York from 29 April to 10 May. These working papers, submitted to the PrepCom by the Islamic Republic of Iran and The People's Republic of China, are re-published from the website of the United Nations Office of Disarmament Affairs which contains many other relavent submissions.

1. The Islamic Republic of Iran, pursuant to article VII of the Treaty on the Non-Proliferation of Nuclear Weapons, supports efforts to establish nuclear-weapon-free zones and believes that such zones are not an end in themselves but rather a means to an end, i.e. contributing to the nuclear non-proliferation objective and enhancing global and regional peace and security.

2. The Islamic Republic of Iran attaches great importance to, and strongly supports, the establishment of a nuclear-weapon-free zone in the Middle East, an initiative which was originally presented by Iran in 1974.

3. Consistent with this principled position, Iran has already taken various practical steps aimed at making progress towards, *inter alia*, the establishment of a Middle East zone free of nuclear weapons and other weapons of mass destruction, in particular by becoming a party to all international legally binding instruments on weapons of mass destruction.[1] Such a high record of accession testifies to the strong commitment of the Islamic Republic of Iran to achieving the objective of the prohibition of the development, production, stockpiling, use or threat of use of weapons of mass destruction, in the Middle East in particular and at the global level in general.

4. The adoption, by the 1995 Review and Extension Conference of the Parties to the Non-Proliferation Treaty, of the resolution on the Middle East, as an essential and integral element of the outcome of the 1995 Review and Extension Conference and of the basis on which the Treaty was indefinitely extended without a vote in 1995 marks a turning point in advancing the proposal for the establishment of a nuclear-weapon-free zone in the Middle East. The Islamic Republic of Iran has always supported and called for the speedy implementation of this resolution and the full realization of its objective in establishing such a zone.

5. Iran also supported the adoption of the 2010 plan of action on the implementation of the 1995 resolution on the Middle East, which called for the convening of a conference in 2012 on the establishment of a Middle East zone free of nuclear weapons and all other weapons of mass destruction. On 6 November 2012, Iran officially declared its decision to participate in that conference, which had been scheduled to be held in December 2012 in Helsinki.

6. However, not only was the 2010 plan of action on the implementation of the 1995 resolution on the Middle East not implemented and, consequently, the 2012 conference not convened, but in addition, the 2015 Review Conference of the Parties to the Non-Proliferation Treaty was unable to reach an agreement on its outcome document as a result of the objection of only the United States of America, the United Kingdom of Great Britain and Northern Ireland and Canada to a decision contained therein on the implementation of the 2010 plan of action on the Middle East.

7. Now, 24 years after the adoption of the 1995 resolution on the Middle East and 9 years after the adoption of the 2010 action plan for the

implementation of that resolution, and despite the strong support of the overwhelming majority of the States parties, as well as the efforts by Iran and all Arab countries in the region for their implementation, there are valid questions: why were they not implemented, and why have all efforts under the 2005 and 2015 Review Conferences for their implementation failed? The answer is clear: the Israeli regime, which is the only non-party to the Treaty and also the only possessor of nuclear weapons in the region, is the main obstacle to the establishment of such a zone. In addition, in practice, certain parties to the Treaty, by representing the Israeli regime in the Treaty's Review Conferences, object to decisions on the actual realization of this zone. One day after the conclusion of the 2010 Review Conference of the Parties to the Non-Proliferation Treaty, the Israeli regime, in its statement dated 29 May 2010, rejected outright the Final Document of that Conference as "deeply flawed" and stated that "Israel will not be able to take part in its implementation."

8. The Final Document of the 2010 Review Conference called on all States to refrain from undertaking any measures that preclude the achievement of the objective of the 1995 resolution on the Middle East. However, the United States, as one of the co-sponsors of the 1995 resolution and as one of the co-conveners of the 2012 conference, by supporting the obstructive positions of the Israeli regime and setting preconditions for the implementation of the 2010 action plan, acted as a stumbling block in the way of convening the 2012 conference and, on 23 November 2012, unilaterally announced that the conference could not be convened and that it would not support a conference in which Israel would be subject to pressure or isolation. This unilateral decision of the United States was wholly inconsistent with its declaratory commitment to the implementation of the 1995 resolution on the Middle East.

9. Subsequently, during the 2015 Review Conference, Israeli officials expressed concern over taking any decision by the Conference "to force Israel to come clean on its nuclear capabilities" as an essential step towards establishing a nuclear-weapon-free zone in the Middle East. In order to avoid that, Israel placed the United States under pressure to block such a decision. When the United States, along with the United Kingdom and Canada, objected to the adoption of the draft outcome document of the Conference, which contained a decision on the implementation of the 1995 resolution and the 2010 action plan on the

Middle East, the Prime Minister of Israel thanked the United States President for such action.

10. But why was the Israeli regime not willing to support the establishment of a nuclear-weapon-free zone in the Middle East, and why is it still not willing to do so? First and foremost, it is because this regime possesses nuclear weapons and other weapons of mass destruction and the establishment of a nuclear-weapon-free zone in the Middle East requires the prompt and unconditional accession of Israel, as a non-nuclear weapon party, to the Non-Proliferation Treaty, renouncing possession of nuclear weapons and placing all of its clandestine nuclear activities and facilities under the comprehensive safeguards of the International Atomic Energy Agency (IAEA).

11. Moreover, a short look at the practices of the Israeli regime in the Middle East and its record in the fields of disarmament and international security provides a clear picture of the seriousness of the security threat posed by this regime against the peace and security of the States parties to the Treaty in the Middle East. It also proves, once again, how essential and urgent the establishment of a Middle East zone free of nuclear and all other weapons of mass destruction is for the maintenance of peace and security in the region and beyond. That record includes, but is not limited to, the following: since its inception, the Israeli regime has waged 17 wars, which means one war almost every four years; committed aggression against all of its neighbours, without exception; even attacked several other non-neighbouring countries in the region and beyond; attacked, in 1981, the peaceful nuclear installations of a State party to the Treaty in the Middle East (in this case, the Security Council strongly condemned the military attack by Israel as a clear violation of the Charter of the United Nations and the norms of international conduct); threatened to attack the peaceful nuclear facilities of States parties to the Treaty in the region that are under the IAEA safeguards; has recently threatened a party to the Treaty in the region with nuclear annihilation; still has under occupation the territories of several neighbouring countries, as it is called, in United Nations resolutions, the "occupying Power"; is not party to the Non-Proliferation Treaty or any other international instrument banning weapons of mass destruction, in defiance of repeated calls, including by the Security Council, the General Assembly, the General Conference of the IAEA, the Review Conferences of the Parties to the Non-

Proliferation Treaty, the summits and ministerial conferences of the Non-Aligned Movement and the Organization of Islamic Cooperation; and is the only possessor of all types of weapons of mass destruction, including hundreds of nuclear warheads, in the Middle East.

12. In addition, such realities make it completely clear that the only way to establish a nuclear-weapon-free zone in the Middle East is for the international community to exert and maintain sustained pressure on the Israeli regime to compel it to accede, promptly and unconditionally, as a non-nuclear-weapon party, to the Non-Proliferation Treaty, and to place all of its nuclear activities and installations under the full-scope IAEA safeguards. This approach was acknowledged by the 2000 and 2010 Review Conferences, which reaffirmed "the importance of Israel's accession to the Non-Proliferation Treaty and the placement of all its nuclear facilities under comprehensive IAEA safeguards, in realizing the goal of universal adherence to the Treaty in the Middle East".

13. The Islamic Republic of Iran expresses its deep concern over the persistent and long delay in the implementation of the 1995 resolution and the lack of any progress in the implementation of the respective plan of action of the 2010 Review Conference. Iran stresses that, as reaffirmed by the successive Review Conferences of the Treaty since 1995, the resolution remains valid until its goals and objectives are achieved. This, without doubt, is the individual and collective responsibility of all States parties to the Treaty, in particular the nuclear-weapon States, especially the three depositary States of the Treaty that co-sponsored the 1995 resolution on the Middle East. It should be recalled that the conclusions and recommendations for follow-on actions of the 2010 Review Conference had clearly stipulated that "the States parties renew their resolve to undertake, individually and collectively, all necessary measures aimed at its prompt implementation."

14. In this context and given the above-mentioned considerations, the third session of the Preparatory Committee for the 2020 Review Conference should recommend:

    (a)   Establishing a subsidiary body under Main Committee II of the 2020 Review Conference to consider the urgent implementation of the 1995 resolution and the 2010 plan of action on the Middle East and, building upon past experience, agree on concrete steps for their speedy implementation;

(b) Noting the consensus reached by the General Assembly since its thirty-fifth session that the establishment of a nuclear-weapon-free zone in the region of the Middle East would greatly enhance international peace and security;

(c) Expressing concern about the lack of progress towards the implementation of the resolution on the Middle East adopted by the 1995 Review and Extension Conference, as well as the action plan on the Middle East adopted at the 2010 Review Conference;

(d) Reaffirming the urgent need for the prompt and full implementation of the 1995 resolution and the 2010 plan of action on the Middle East;

(e) Reiterating the firm commitment of all States parties to the Treaty, and in particular the nuclear-weapon States, to undertake all necessary measures aimed at the prompt and full implementation of the 1995 resolution and the 2010 plan of action on the Middle East and to extend their cooperation in this regard;

(f) Emphasizing the essential role of the United Nations in the establishment of a nuclear-weapon-free zone in the Middle East;

(g) Expressing serious concern about the continued existence in the Middle East of unsafeguarded nuclear facilities, as well as the threat posed by the proliferation of nuclear weapons to the security and stability of the Middle East;

(h) Expressing deepest concern over the fact that the refusal of Israel is the main obstacle to the implementation of the 1995 resolution and the 2010 plan of action on the Middle East;

(i) Reaffirming the importance of the accession of Israel to the Non-Proliferation Treaty without precondition and further delay and the placement of all of its nuclear activities and facilities under the comprehensive IAEA safeguards, in realizing the goal of universal adherence to the Treaty in the Middle East;

(j) Urging Israel to renounce possession of nuclear

weapons and to place all of its unsafeguarded nuclear facilities under the full-scope IAEA safeguards as an important confidence-building measure among all States of the region and as a step towards enhancing peace and security;

(k) Reaffirming the commitment of all States parties to the effective prohibition of the transfer of all nuclear-related equipment, information, materials and facilities, resources or devices and the extension of know-how or any kind of assistance in the nuclear, scientific or technological fields to Israel so long as it remains a non-party to the Treaty and has not placed all of its nuclear activities and facilities under the full-scope IAEA safeguards;

(l) Deciding to establish a standing committee, comprising the members of its Bureau, to follow up on the implementation of the recommendations of the Review Conference concerning the prompt accession of Israel to the Non-Proliferation Treaty and the placement of all of its nuclear activities and facilities under the full-scope IAEA safeguards, and to report to the 2025 Review Conference and its Preparatory Committee meetings.

Note:

1. The Islamic Republic of Iran is a party to the Protocol for the Prohibition of the Use in War of Asphyxiating, Poisonous or Other Gases, and of Bacteriological Methods of Warfare (1925 Geneva Protocol), the Treaty on the Non-Proliferation of Nuclear Weapons, the Convention on the Prohibition of the Development, Production and Stockpiling of Bacteriological (Biological) and Toxin Weapons and on Their Destruction and the Convention on the Prohibition of the Development, Production, Stockpiling and Use of Chemical Weapons and on Their Destruction, as well as a signatory to the Comprehensive Nuclear-Test-Ban Treaty. Iran has also concluded a safeguards agreement with the International Atomic Energy Agency for the application of safeguards in connection with the Treaty on the Non-proliferation of Nuclear Weapons.

* * *

In 2018, the UN General Assembly asked the Secretary General to convene in 2019 a conference on establishing a zone free of nuclear weapons and all other weapons of mass destruction (WMDFZ) in the Middle East.

2. Nuclear disarmament

Working paper submitted by China

1. The complete prohibition and thorough destruction of nuclear weapons, with the ultimate attainment of a nuclear-weapon-free world, serve the common interests of mankind and constitute a shared aspiration of all countries.

2. Today, the international security environment is undergoing a complex array of profound changes, with existing international arms control and non-proliferation system brought under severe strain. Cold war mentality has resurged as the prism through which some major country assesses international security environment and the basis for the formulation of its strategic security polices. The world is confronted with a critical choice between unilateralism and multilateralism, confrontation and dialogue, isolation and openness, zero-sum game and win-win progress. The international community is generally concerned about the exacerbating international environment.

China believes that, under current circumstances, it is ever more important to underline the conducive role that the consistent nuclear disarmament progress could play in improving international security environment, and is more pertinent than ever for all countries to jointly champion multilateralism, oppose and discard cold war mentality, and to uphold the authority and effectiveness of the multilateral mechanism with the NPT included. Over the years, US-Russia bilateral nuclear disarmament agreement have contributed to international peace and security. Joint efforts by nuclear weapon States to preserve the authority of NPT and the rule-based international order, as well as persistent fulfillment of their obligations under those bilateral and multilateral arms control agreements to which they are parties, will make great contributions to continued improvement of the international security environment.

3. With this understanding, China has the following viewpoints:
    I)   Bear in mind the historical responsibility of building a community of shared future for mankind through consultation and joint efforts, promote the building of a new form of international relations characterized by mutual respect, fairness, justice and win-win

cooperation, uphold a concept of common, comprehensive, cooperative and sustainable security, fully respect and accommodate the legitimate and reasonable security concerns for all states, and strive to build a peaceful and stable international security environment.

II) Take fair and reasonable nuclear disarmament steps of gradual reduction towards a downward balance, relevant measures should follow the principles of "maintaining global strategic stability" and "undiminished security for all". Countries possessing the largest nuclear arsenals bear special and primary responsibility for nuclear disarmament and should continue to make drastic and substantive reductions in their nuclear arsenals in a verifiable, irreversible and legally binding manner while faithfully implementing their existing nuclear arms reduction treaties. This would create necessary conditions for other nuclear-weapon states to join in multilateral negotiations on nuclear disarmament.

III) Diminish the role of nuclear weapons in national security doctrines, and abandon the policies of nuclear deterrence based on the first-use of nuclear weapons. **All nuclear-weapon states should commit to no-first-use of nuclear weapons unconditionally, and conclude international legal instruments in this regard.** The historic process of banning biological and chemical weapons shows that "no-first-use" is the most practical, feasible and valuable means of nuclear disarmament at present.

IV) All nuclear-weapon States should commit themselves to the effective implementation of Article 6 of the NPT, abide by the outcomes of previous NPT Review Conferences, and openly declare that they have no intention to seek permanent possession of nuclear weapons. Relevant nuclear-weapon States should put an end to the policy and practice of nuclear umbrella and nuclear sharing, and withdraw all nuclear weapons that are deployed in other countries. **Building nuclear-weapon-free zones is an important step towards realizing a nuclear-weapon-free world.** Nuclear-weapon States should support in a more active manner the efforts by non-nuclear-weapon states to build nuclear-weapon-free zones on the basis of consultations among themselves and voluntary agreements.

V) The three pillars of NPT, i.e. Nuclear disarmament, nuclear non-proliferation and peaceful use of nuclear energy are complementing each other and should not be partially neglected. The international community should promote the three pillars in a comprehensive and balanced manner, oppose double standards, maintain and strengthen the authority, universality and effectiveness of the treaty.

4. As a nuclear-weapon State, China has never evaded its responsibility, and has earnestly been fulfilling its obligation of nuclear disarmament, strictly adhered to the outcomes of previous NPT Review Conferences, and made sincere contributions to promoting nuclear disarmament through concrete actions.

- China remains committed to the path of peaceful development, adhering to a nuclear strategy of self-defense, and upholding an open, transparent and responsible nuclear policy.
- China has never deployed any nuclear weapons abroad, has never participated in nuclear arms race of any kind, nor will China participate in the future. China's nuclear force is always kept at the minimal level required by national security.
- China undertakes not to be the first to use nuclear weapons at any time and under any circumstances, and unconditionally commits itself not to use or threaten to use nuclear weapons against non-nuclear-weapon States or nuclear-weapon-free zones. This is the most transparent policy, and the most consistent commitment.
- China supports the early entry into force of the Comprehensive Nuclear-Test-Ban, and has strictly observed its commitment to a moratorium on nuclear testing. China is making steady progress in domestic preparation for the implementation of the Treaty. A batch of IMS monitoring stations in China has been certified by the PTS, highlighting China's firm support to the Treaty.
- China supports the early commencement of negotiation on FMCT under the framework of the Conference on Disarmament,

on the basis of an agreement on a comprehensive and balanced program of work, pursuant to the Shannon Report (CD/1299) and the mandate contained therein. The United Nations FMCT High-Level Preparatory Group has accomplished its mission, and China supports the CD to establish the subsidiary body to continue relevant technical discussions.

- China supports all sides to have frank, practical and meaningful dialogues on international security environment, global strategic stability, reducing risks of nuclear war, etc., within the existing regime.
- China values the constructive dialogues with non-nuclear-weapon states, and fully understands the good will of non-nuclear-weapon States to speed up international nuclear disarmament. China stands ready to maintain communication and engagement with non-nuclear-weapon States with a view to preserving and strengthening the current nuclear disarmament mechanism, and to achieving the ultimate goal of a world free of nuclear weapons with a step-by-step approach.

5. China will continue to play an active and constructive role in enhancing unity and cooperation of the international community, advancing the common cause of nuclear disarmament, and promoting international peace and stability.

Reviews

Over the Wall

Nicholas J. Barnett, *Britain's Cold War: Culture, Modernity, and the Soviet Threat*, I.B. Tauris, 2018, 292 pages, hardback ISBN 9781784538057, £99

Nine chapters, crisply written, frequently sardonic, book-ended by Introduction and Conclusion, fortified by 30 pages of terse supplementary end-notes, 7-part Bibliography (ignoring electronic sources), 8-page lacunose Index, 22 black-white illustrations, many Vicky cartoons — splendid to see these biting caricatures again. The book is accurately printed, apart from pages 227 and 241, which give discrepant dates (1964/1965) for Khrushchev's downfall.

'Innovative exciting new insights …' Blurb by Joe Moran, Barnett's PhD supervisor — He Would Say That, Wouldn't He?

No mention of *Britain's Cold War* (2012), one of several books by archaeologist-historian Bob Clarke, with cognate attention to defensive nuclear architecture.

Barnett's termini are 1951-65, making little sense. Cold War had long been in full swing, down to Reagan's 'Tear Down that Wall!' and Mrs Thatcher 'doing business' with Gorbachev. Thanks to Putin and Trump, it is back with a vengeance.

1956 might have been focused as watershed: Khrushchev's 'Secret Speech'; Suez and Hungary; British visit by 'Bulge and Krush'. Barnett here mentions Nye Bevan clashing with Khrushchev, but not his spectacular ('I'd vote Conservative') slanging-match with the (as usual) 'tired and emotional' George Brown. He devotes five pages (92-97) to the farcical incident of hat-stealing discus thrower Nina Pomonareva, nary a word about the mysterious disappearance of frogman Buster Crabb (regarded by some as the model for Bond). Still, it hardly matters, in that Barnett leaps his own chronological boundaries in both directions, from the 1930s until today.

Barnett announces five major, recurrent themes. First, Eastern Europe as a monolithic detached entity, which he rightly challenges: consider the differences between (say) Albania, Yugoslavia, and East Germany. Second, the role of religion in the 'cultural conflict', stressing the Apocalyptic side, correctly traced back to early Church Schisms. Third, interplay between 'tradition and modernity', exemplified through nuclear and space science.

So far, so good. The fourth and fifth propositions are dubious. Especially the former, harping on the 'role of masculinity in the cultural cold war'. Barnett is obsessed with this, the term (and cognates) recurrent beyond counting, frequently multiple times per page, adducing such absurd articles as Brian Baker's 'Masculinity and Food in the spy fiction of Len Deighton'. Not until the end (p.239) does Barnett remember Rosa Klebb and other unspecified — think *Modesty Blaise* — female agents.

The fifth involves the 'narrow range of publishable ideological positions', an idea adopted from some predecessors. Not everyone 'treated the *Daily Worker* with suspicion or disdain', the entire body of conflicting Trotskyist analyses (notably Tony Cliff) is ignored, and the notion violates Barnett's own correct signalling of humour as a weapon, from Vicky to the 'Red Dean of Canterbury' and John Osborne's silly 'Damn You, England', *Tribune* (August 18, 1961).

Hewlett-Johnson takes a pasting in chapters one and nine, ridiculing (p.117) his ' bizarre cult' (re Hungary), and branding his notorious pamphlet, *The Socialist Sixth of the World,* as 'bought for grim amusement'. I'd have contrasted him with Donald Soper, one of Harold Wilson's Methodists, albeit he offered qualified support for Soviet communism and when asked what he'd do if Russia invaded, replied 'welcome them with a cup of tea'.

Incidentally, when involved with Healy's Socialist Labour League, I recall Cliff Slaughter demanding that its monthly *Labour Review* cease giving books to 'that silly old fool Soper' — such was the Healyite notion of free speech.

Barnett maintains his promise to spotlight lesser-known novels by devoting chapters 1 and 9 to Paul Winterton's *Murder in Moscow* and *Ashes of Lada*, chapter 6 to Maurice Edelman's (Labour MP) *Call on Kuprin*, not nowadays household names.

Bigger ones naturally offset these. Orwell dominates. Rightly so; he coined the expression 'Cold War', *Tribune* October 19, 1945. At their different levels, Deighton, Fleming, Le Carré (should have quoted his 'There's a theory in the Service that Etonians are discreet'), Greene, though no mention of his forgotten *It's a Battlefield*, wherein the Communist Party of Great Britain (CPGB) tries to manoeuvre a hanging to make a political martyr.

Various transitions gleam. Greene would later controversially uphold Philby and Russia over America. Contrast Kingsley Amis, moving from CPGB membership to ardent Thatcherite, here manifest in his *Russian*

Hide and Seek (Mrs Thatcher chided him for 'getting the wrong side'). Also High Tory Anthony Powell, who focused his satire equally on CPGB's Gypsy Jones vending *Peace Now!* and middle-class Trotskyites.

Barnett casts a wide net across cinema, television, theatre, wireless. Might have noticed that *On the Beach* had been anticipated by Hollywood's 1955 *The Day the World Ended*. Fun to see such boyhood heroes as Dan Dare (add *Journey into Space*) and Dick Barton exhumed. Also the preposterous *High Treason* (1951) with its CPGB saboteurs coaxed by female Soviet agent, plus its predecessor *Seven Days to Noon*, wherein a pacifist nuclear professor steals an atomic device and threatens to blow up London to back his demand for Disarmament. Also evokes Bond's *obiter dictum*: 'the most deadly saboteur in the world — the little man with the heavy suitcase'.

Chapters 2 and 7 focus the threat of nuclear annihilation and disarmament/peace movements; see now Peter Hennessy's new book, *Winds of Change: Britain in the Early Sixties* (2019). Bertrand Russell's role is strangely minimized, his speeches, writings, and arrest passed over. The rival 'Balance of Terror' argument was flirted with by Attlee and (reluctantly) Orwell, passionately espoused by Gaitskell ('Fight, Fight, and Fight Again') and Nye Bevan ('Naked into the Conference Chamber'). For the CND mix of Christians and Communists and the CPGB's ambivalence, see Jeremy Tranmer's online essay. Much also on Civil Defence, focusing Coventry Labour council's abandonment (defeatism or realism?) and *Beyond the Fringe's* (oddly classified as a novel) hilarious sketch on its official brochure's absurdities.

Chapters 5 and 8 cover the Space Race. British Sputnik coverage was inevitably dominated by sympathy for space-dog Laika. The mood changed for Yuri Gagarin's visit (1961, one month before the Berlin Wall). What if 'Little Lemon' Laika had been sent? Alas. it was the dog that died, as would Gagarin in a mysterious aeroplane crash. Demands (eg by Marjorie Proops) for a female cosmonaut were answered by Russia's Valentina Tereschkova (1963). Barnett beat me to it by suggesting British fears of deep space exploration were prompted by TV's *The Quatermass Experiment*, watched by the whole country in 1953.

Two simple facts: America beat the Russians to the Moon. America is the only country to have used nuclear bombs.

Chapter 3 encompasses the post-Stalin 'Thaw' and friendlier Western perceptions, copiously illustrated by Henri Cartier-Bresson's 1954 photographs. Probably a shock to professional anti-communists that Russia contained millions of ordinary people living ordinary lives. *Picture*

Post's serialization of *Animal* Farm was blatant counter-propaganda. Barnett (p. 84) goes easy on the plight of Russian homosexuals, criminalized by Stalin, repressed until 1993; see Rustam Alexander's online PhD thesis. We can also brighten his gloomy litany of British football defeats by recalling Wolves' victories over Moscow Spartak (4-0) and Budapest Honved (3-2).

Chapters 4 and 8 examine the black spots of Hungary (1956) and Berlin Wall (1961) — the 1953 East German uprising is elided, whilst on Suez I'll only say that Eden would have done better to help Russia build the Aswan Dam. Matyas Rakosi's sacking and the ill-fated Imre Nagy crop up, though not Janos Kadar, hailed in Western circles as a ' liberaliser', though I once met a Hungarian artist who judged him worse than Rakosi. The familiar Hungarian facts are (with Vicky's aid) expertly delineated. As to the discomfitures of the 'egregious' Red Dean and the CPGB, Barnett kindles an impressive bonfire of their inanities. I will intrude three personal memories:

1. Seeing the then Trotskyist John Daniels Senior confront CPGB member John Peck in Nottingham's Slab Square;
2. Listening to Peter Fryer retailing the eyewitness accounts the *Daily Worker* would not print (shades of *Homage to Catalonia's* fate).
3. My Stalinist father who claimed the 'soft' hands of Hungarian r efugees on television proved they were not 'real workers'.

Barnett's detailed treatment of the Berlin Wall and receptions to it is echoed in the last sentence of his Conclusion, after a general wrap-up, final return to Orwell, a spotlight on Apocalypticism, and plea for more study of John (misspelled 'Jon') Bryan's novel *The Man Who Came Back* (1958, stressing female Cold War activities):

' When Britons looked through the Iron Curtain they saw Big Brother, but they also saw a population who were quite like them.'

Overall, Barnett's book is a well-documented, perceptive, highly readable narrative, comporting vivid memories for those of us who were there and rich enlightenment for those who were not.

Barry Baldwin

Common European Home

Eckart Conze, Martin Klimke and Jeremy Varon, *Nuclear Threats, Nuclear Fear and the Cold War of the 1980s*, **Cambridge University Press, 2017, 370 pages, hardback ISBN 9781107136281, £99.99**

'END' means different things to different people. The idea and political project that became European Nuclear Disarmament emerged in discussions between Ralph Miliband, Ken Coates, Stuart Holland, Mary Kaldor, Edward Thompson and others. In late 1979, according to Ken Coates in *Listening for Peace* (Spokesman, 1987), Edward had written to Tony Benn MP seeking his help in mobilizing 'civil disobedience against the projected new nuclear bases' for US cruise and Pershing missiles in six European NATO member states including the UK. Edward sent Ken copies of his letters. 'But Benn did not at the time believe that he could meet Edward's precise request,' wrote Ken. 'It was at this point that I rang Edward to propose, instead of a purely national response, we should seek to create a European answer. The formula which had escaped us hitherto was absolutely simple: we should seek to create a nuclear-free zone in all of Europe.'

But the context for this 'European answer' lay deeper. Ken Coates wrote that the Bertrand Russell Peace Foundation 'had been seeking a basis upon which to associate a European peace movement ever since 1974, when we convened a seminar at Bradford under the title *The Just Society*', which addressed the divisions between communism and social democracy in Europe, taking a paper by the Russian historian, Roy Medvedev, as its starting point. Eduard Goldstücker, the exiled Czech writer and 1968 Prague Spring activist, suggested that the

> 'impasse in relations between East and West Europe, and the adverse conditions of work suffered by independent socialist thinkers in the East, were intricately related and that only a new and comprehensive European peace movement could open any possibility for a real change for the better.'

This idea took hold, but it was some years before it surfaced in the guise of END. Edward Thompson had also participated in the Bradford seminar.

Further back, the Bertrand Russell Peace Foundation was formed in 1963, in the aftermath of the Cuban Missile Crisis, in which Khrushchev used Russell's letters to conduct something of a public campaign in relation to Kennedy to dial down from nuclear confrontation. During the 1960s, the US war on Vietnam was a major priority for the Foundation, including the International War Crimes Tribunal, launched in 1966. There were sustained campaigns on Africa, Palestine, and for the release of Soviet Jews who wished to live in Israel. 'Transnational' work was the Foundation's daily occupation, with Russell's active participation until his death in 1970. Sustained campaigns to uphold human rights were central. For example, in the wake of the Soviet invasion of Czechoslovakia in 1968, there was a long campaign addressed to the international postal authorities to uphold Alexander Dubcek's right to engage in international correspondence. Years later, in 1989, as Chair of its Human Rights Committee, Ken Coates welcomed Mr Dubcek to the European Parliament to receive the Sakharov Prize for Freedom of Thought.

Back in 1980, Edward Thompson rightly commented that the Russell Foundation had an extensive European address book. In fact, there were also many addresses beyond Europe, in Asia, the Americas and elsewhere. When Edward first drafted what became the END Appeal, the return address was Gamble Street, Nottingham, which was inundated with mail from far and wide. These were the Russell Foundation's offices, shared with the Russell Press, which printed *Protest and Survive*, Edward's counterblast to the Thatcher Government's 'protect and survive' civil defence 'codology' against nuclear attack. The movement grew rapidly, and I was recruited to help Ken Fleet, secretary of the Foundation and, later with Ken Coates, joint secretary of the END Liaison Committee, which organised the END Conventions, beginning in Brussels in 1982. Earlier, in summer 1981, we marched from Copenhagen to Paris (or, at least, part of the way) with the Nordic Women for Peace, for a nuclear-weapons-free Europe. Edward joined us.

I rehearse this history as a counterweight to Patrick Burke's account in 'END Transnational Peace Campaigning in the 1980s'. Patrick's starting point is the END office in London, which eventually gave rise to a membership organisation in Britain. As he says in a footnote, 'the British group END was not referred to at the time as British END; I do so here in order to distinguish it from the END Convention and the END Convention Liaison Committee'.

Meanwhile, the END idea or process spread. Looking back, the split between the Russell Foundation and 'British END' probably proved rather productive. Why the split happened is another story, but much emotional energy and writing paper were saved for more constructive purposes. The Russell Foundation focused on the END Conventions, which met annually, while 'British END' developed its own priorities, particularly contacts with individuals and groups in what were then still member states of the Warsaw Pact. Patrick describes these in some detail.

The Berlin END Convention in 1983 represented something of a high-water mark, from the perspective of a 'real change for the better' sought at Bradford in 1974. The Soviet Peace Committee had launched a public broadside against the planned Convention, after meeting with the German organisers. Reunification of divided Germany figured in the emerging agenda for the Berlin Convention, and this was, for some, a step too far. Whilst in Berlin, I phoned Roy Medvedev in Moscow to record his supportive message to the Convention. Petra Kelly of the German Greens participated, as did Oskar Lafontaine of the SPD. We joined hands around the vast International Congress Centre, where the Convention met. At the end, Ken Coates had to return early to England as Mrs Thatcher had announced a General Election in which he was to be an unsuccessful candidate.

In 1984, Ken again stood unsuccessfully for election, this time to the European Parliament. Eventually, in 1989, he was elected and, along with activists Peter Crampton and Michael McGowan, END went to the European Parliament in Brussels and Strasbourg. Gorbachev was General Secretary of the Communist Party of the Soviet Union, and had paid attention to the mass peace movements of the 1980s, as he had the Russell-Einstein Manifesto of 1955, urging scientists to alert the world to nuclear dangers, which he had heard as a student in Prague. Lawrence Wittner refers to this in his contribution to the book under review. In 1986, Gorbachev had negotiated the Intermediate-range Nuclear Forces Treaty with President Reagan. Subsequently, 'glasnost' and 'perestroika' became common parlance.

To encourage constructive, democratic change, Ken Coates with others urged a joint meeting between the European Parliament and the Supreme Soviet, and active preparations were under way for what would have been a groundbreaking meeting. Ken understood such a project as very much within the spirit of END. But Gorbachev's fall in 1991 put paid to such audacious plans to safeguard our common European home from the nuclear threat.

Tony Simpson

Plucking the orchid

Ocean Vuong, *On Earth We're Briefly Gorgeous*, Jonathan Cape 2019, 242 pages, ISBN 9781787331501, £12.99

For a moment, in the primal scene that inaugurates Ocean Vuong's debut collection *Night Sky with Exit Wounds*, identity slips its cultural moorings and pulls us in to the glistening voyeurism of body confronting body, enraptured son and imaginary father, or lover, or lyre-bearing Orpheus: *the man showering, ... the rain falling through him: guitar strings snapping / over his globed shoulders ... I didn't know / the cost of entering a song – was to lose / your way back.* Similarly, Statovci's first novel *My Cat Yugoslavia* [2014] begins with its Kosovar Albanian protagonist trawling the internet for a homosexual hook-up which, in night time Helsinki, follows on almost instantaneously and is celebrated in the most ardent, rawly evocative terms. A single poem or chapter later, however, the magnetic pull of what Joseph Brodsky disparagingly calls the 'retrospective and retroactive' mechanism of the writer in exile, or Edward Said more sympathetically a 'contrapuntalism' attendant on 'terminal loss', has in both cases asserted itself. Vuong's pages rehearse, through images of bombed cathedrals, bullet holes and burning cities (the fall of Saigon), all the psychological detritus of a war zone his family carries with it to the America of *Briefly Gorgeous*; Statovci documents with a dogged realism, lugubrious and censorious, the patriarchal mores, arranged weddings and domestic slavery of the rural world near Priština as Yugoslavia disintegrates into ethnic conflict and genocide. Disclaimers apart, and Statovci – assimilated into Finnish society from the age of two — has explicitly rejected the classification, the essential dichotomy running through immigrant or exilic literature couldn't be more starkly evidenced, between personal acts of transcendence, here eroticised but also, perhaps more profoundly, imaginative or *literary*, and the scale and anonymity of the mass phenomenon itself.

Thus Brodsky's and Said's classic 1980s reflections assemble an illustrious high cultural pedigree that stretches from Ovid to Dante, Conrad, Joyce and ultimately, one supposes, themselves, but whose relationship to the wider anguish, for both, engenders serious moral unease. 'As we gather here, in this attractive and well-lit room [Getty-Wiedenfeld-sponsored Wheatland Conference, Vienna], on this cold December evening, to discuss the plight of the writer in exile, let us pause for a minute and think of some of those who, quite naturally, didn't make it', Brodsky taunts his fellow illuminati. Then, more confrontationally, 'whether he likes it or not, *Gastarbeiters* and refugees of any stripe effectively pluck the orchid out of an exiled writer's lapel'. *We are now witnessing the highest levels of displacement on record ... 70.8 million people around the world have been forced from home. Among them are nearly 25.9 million refugees* [UNHCR UK 2019]: how can the isolated consciousness justify its wrestle with the conventions of literary discourse in the face of *that*? Gazmend Kapllani's *Short Border Handbook* [2006], a product of the Albanian generation immediately preceding Statovci's, acts out the conundrum by dividing each of its chapters into two irreconcilable halves – a gruelling linear odyssey of the demonization and exploitation of large numbers of impoverished male refugees at the hands of their Greek neighbours post-Hoxha; and a series of Kundera-style miniature essays that analyse, with pointed irony and philosophical sophistication, the migrant experience as a whole. The stand-off is broken at two points only: first as farce, when the émigré-narrator's visit to a bookstore selling Marquez and Borges, at a very late stage in the text, suddenly alerts the reader to his true personal trajectory – and coincides with the onset of a truncheon-wielding police action that thrusts him back into the throng at their most abject and dehumanised. Later, a passing Greek film maker who knows Kadare and senses an intellectual affinity whisks him off to Athens and journalistic-media stardom ['being an immigrant means ... exposing yourself to the extreme games of fate'], but not before the separate worlds of the drowned and the saved have been placed before us, one last time, in all their intractable alterity:

> 'From the window, I caught sight of a human caravan – my fellow countrymen ... like weary shadows walking without direction, like ghosts roaming around in the night ... I felt a river of tears rushing down my throat and I broke into sobs'.

Crossing, like its gentler predecessor, pursues the chimeras of sexual transcendence and geographical relocation but with an almost pathological (indeed, murderous) intensity. Zelig-like in the slippage between multiple identities, the central character, Bujar, who calls himself a 'compulsive liar', is ready to adopt as alternatives to the only other option refugee isolation and introversion offer him, attempted suicide. As the exquisite, rhapsodically physical, always evanescent intimacies pile up, the visceral rejection of Kosovo's 'cavemen' mentality now transfers to Tirana, Durrës and by implication the entire homeland, its comprehensive derilection and bloated nationalist fantasies, and Finnish xenophobia is replaced by Rome's sunlit complacency and New York's 'stony heart', endemic racism and economic ruthlessness (one balks at the stereotypes, unsure whether one is supposed to). Said warns against a

> 'kind of narcissistic masochism that resists all efforts at amelioration, acculturation, and community ... To live as if everything around you were temporary and perhaps trivial is to fall prey to petulant cynicism as well as querulous lovelessness ...'

But Bujar, force-fed as a child the mythic origins and folklore of Albanian heroism, exploited by traffickers, sexual predators and reality TV producers, is also the quintessential victim of a systemic atrocity whose return from exile, empty-handed, to the unchanging beggardom of his origins – 'a tattered mattress on the floor wrapped in a white sheet and black curtains pulled across the windows'- has a universalising pathos. Meanwhile Bujar's queerness, and that of the boyhood companions, drag queens and trans women who form his emotional and psychological lifeline, represents a further step in the dismantling of the regional homophobia begun, for some commentators, with *My Cat Yugoslavia* and a necessary corrective to the bloody machismo embodied, at the end of this novel, by Skanderbeg.

For Vuong victimhood is never a given, nor is it the predetermined outcome. Yes, the impossible weight of numbers of those eternally on the move means that

> 'some monarchs, on their way south, simply stop flying, their wings all of a sudden too heavy – and fall away, deleting themselves from the story ...'

Yes, at its most delusory the refugee's hopeful freedom in the interim between countries may be little more than

> 'the [veal] calf's wide pupils as the latch is opened, and it charges from its prison toward the man with a harness ready to loop around its neck ...'

There's no shortage of such bleak estimates, presented, it has to be said, as incontrovertible fact rather than phenomena one might explain or ameliorate, and the threats from within and without to the precarious protective nucleus of the Vietnamese family's three generations, whose tale/memoir/imaginative reconstruction *Briefly Gorgeous* is, verge consistently, in their horror and virtual omnipresence, on the insurmountable: the grandmother's encounter with an American soldier whose power over her is juxtaposed with a scene of other soldiers consuming the brain, for its aphrodisiac qualities, of a still living macaque monkey; the mother's post-traumatic stress disorder (PTSD) and violent mental disorders; wife beatings; omnipresent, casual and daily racism in the US; the abysmal working conditions, 'aching, toxic, and underpaid', of immigrant labour in nail salons and tobacco plantations. For Little Dog, the narrator, there are the additional travails of white male homophobia and the sense that he owes his very existence to imperialism: '*It wasn't me*, the boy thinks, *who was inside my mother's womb, but this bullet, this seed I bloomed around*'. Overwhelmingly, however, the effect of the novel is to move, unlike Statovci's, cumulatively beyond the self into the 'chance' and 'privilege' of a shared future. Instead of corralling people into tribes viewed contemptuously from a distance, Little Dog builds on the loving nurturing of his upbringing to face outwards towards and make common cause with other underclasses cheated by the fraudulence of the American Dream, the copy of Morrison's *Sula* he carries with him a dog-eared emblem of resistance, the soul and rap of Etta James and 50 Cent's *Many men wish death upon me* superimposed on the memory of his grandmother's Vietnamese lullaby and drag queens singing at a wake, their sexual identities utilised by the community, in a Saigon street. Even white trailer trash, whose squalid and limited circumstances Vuong turns to as a mirror in which Little Dog can view his own, play an essential part in the journey to assimilation and reconciliation: sexual union with his lover Trevor – 'we were two people mining one body, and in doing so, merged, until no corner was left saying I' – is seen not so much as a discrete act of self-pleasuring or fulfilment but as one in a series of epiphanies that lead up to arguably the novel's key pronouncement:

> 'All this time I told myself we were born from war – but I was wrong, Ma. We were born from beauty.'

The ringing affirmation speaks both to a sense of social responsibility and to Vuong's astonishing literary craftsmanship, his insistence on the aesthetic object, its poetic shimmer and multi-facetedness, like something Briefly Gorgeous one could turn slowly in one's hands. Perhaps Said and Brodsky would have approved.

Stephen Winfield

Vincent

Edited by Carol Jacobi, *Van Gogh and Britain*, Tate Publishing, 2019, 240 pages, many colour illustrations, hardback ISBN 9781849766012 £40, paperback ISBN 9781849766029 £25

'Van Gogh Tree', written in blue ink in Bertrand Russell's clear hand, is marked with the letter 'C' on his map of Richmond Park. Above it in Bertie's legend, 'B' marks 'Our wood', while immediately below, 'D' marks 'Our Beech tree'. Evidently, Van Gogh Tree was not Russell property. Edith, Bertie's wife, marked B, C, D and 32 more locations on their map of Richmond Park. 'Sites known to BR in childhood', she wrote on the map's cover, adding 'Marked by ER and verified by BR'.

On the map, Van Gogh Tree appears a solitary specimen on the boundary of Hill Farme, between Humfrey Bennett and Little Heathe, near the Bog Gate in Mortlake Parish. Google Earth shows trees continuing to thrive in the area.

Bertie moved to Pembroke Lodge in Richmond Park in 1876. He had lost both parents before his fourth birthday, and came to live with his paternal grandparents in the park. He spent his formative years there, tutored at home, leaving to go to Cambridge University when he was 18. For him, the park provided 'all kinds of secret places in which it was possible to hide from grown-up people so successfully that there was not the slightest fear of discovery'. 'There were many fine trees,' he wrote in his *Autobiography*, 'oaks, beeches, horse- and Spanish chestnuts, and lime trees, a very beautiful cedar tree, cryptomerias and deodaras presented by Indian princes.' What species was/is the Van Gogh Tree?

During his early teens, Bertie had 'an intense interest in religion and philosophy'. He was taken 'on alternate Sundays to the (Episcopalian) Parish Church at Petersham and to the Presbyterian Church at Richmond'.

So what of Vincent? Van Gogh had moved from The Hague to work in London in May 1873, when he had just turned 20. That month, Bertie had his first birthday. Vincent was to spend much of the next three years in and around London, before returning to the Continent. He was not yet working as an artist, but these years in London were hugely influential in his artistic and social formation. *Van Gogh in Britain*, the book of the recent Tate Britain exhibition, tells the story. Tate Britain Director, Alex Farquharson, sums up *Van Gogh and Britain* as 'the first exhibition to examine both the influence of British art and culture on Van Gogh and his subsequent influence on British art'.

In June 1876, Van Gogh came to live in Isleworth, close to Richmond Park. He was hoping to become an urban preacher: 'should I find anything it will probably be a situation somewhere between minister and missionary, in the suburbs of London among working folk', he wrote. Vincent attended the Richmond Wesleyan Methodist church, where he became a lay preacher, giving his first sermon in October 1876, based on a painting, *God Speed! Pilgrims Setting out for Canterbury* by George Henry Boughton. On 19 November he preached at Petersham, sketching the Methodist chapel in a letter to his brother, Theo. In December that year, Vincent returned to The Netherlands for the Christmas holidays in the company of his sister, Anna, who was also working in England. Vincent never came back to Britain, but he left an enduring legacy, including in Richmond Park.

Van Gogh Tree has many counterparts in Vincent's paintings. He loved to paint trees, as *Van Gogh in Britain* testifies. *Starry Night* sparkles in the memory, however.

Tony Simpson

Stamping ground

Robert Macfarlane, *Underland: A Deep Time Journey*, Hamish Hamilton, 2019, 488 pages, hardback ISBN 9780241143803, £20

Robert Macfarlane returned to Nottingham in May 2019. He had grown up in a Nottinghamshire village, 'not a pit village', and attended Nottingham High School as a teenager. He recalled the headstocks visible across the Old Coalfield, totems of Notts' own extensive underland and those who inhabited it. But Nottingham doesn't figure in an obvious way in this 'deep time journey'.

Robert seemed surprised that he was only now returning to his old stamping ground where, 30 years earlier, he had secreted a jam-jar time capsule in the Nottinghamshire house his family were soon to leave, telling of his 'biggest fear, nuclear war', written in pencil on a notebook page. For he was a child of the 1980s, when fears of 'theatre' nuclear war stalked Europe, giving rise to a massive wave of popular resistance which ultimately led to the Intermediate-range Nuclear Forces Treaty signed by Presidents Gorbachev and Reagan in 1987. This European Nuclear Disarmament campaign was co-ordinated, to some degree, from an old hosiery factory along Forest Road, a hop and a skip from Nottingham High School.

There is an acute sense of conflict in *Underland*. The chapter entitled 'Hollow Land', inspired by treks in and over the Slovenian Highlands, recalls the 'White War', 'a series of battles at the border of Austria-Hungary and Italy' that took place between 1915 and 1918. Ernst Friedrich, in his landmark photographic record *War Against War*, recorded the systemic cruelty visited on the peoples of the Balkans following the assassination of Archduke Franz Ferdinand of Austria-Este in 1914.The killing fields returned during the Second World War, when Yugoslavia was the only occupied country to liberate itself from the Nazis. Remains of the dead, many of them summarily executed, continue to be recovered from sink holes in the karst mountains. Basil Davidson's *Partisan Picture* does not figure in Macfarlane's Select Bibliography, but it is a riveting account of what was at stake as Tito rallied the partisans to harry and, ultimately, to defeat the Nazis and their local collaborators amidst the mountains of Yugoslavia, with some help from the British and others. Old conflicts fester anew in these contested territories.

Robert's return to Nottingham was to give the UNESCO City of Literature Lecture at the Council House. 'Building peace in the minds of men and women' is UNESCO's motto. In its own distinctive way, *Underland* contributes to that never-ending work.

Anthony Lane

Become a subscriber ...
The Spokesman
Journal of the *Bertrand Russell Peace Foundation*

Subscription rates are (for three issues): Individual subscriptions: £20, Individual subscriptions - international: £25, Institutional subscriptions UK - £33 Europe - £38 RoW - £40.

Please send me one subscription, starting with Issue No. ....

I enclose payment of £ ....

Name..

Address
....
....
....
....Postcode ....

Email..

Please return this form with a cheque or money order made payable to 'Bertrand Russell House'. Send to The Spokesman, 5 Churchill Park, Nottingham, England, NG4 2HF.

Payments can be made online at the following websites:
www.spokesmanbooks.com | www.spokesmanbookshop.com